mary emmerling's beach cottages

mary emmerling's beach cottages

AT HOME BY THE SEA

Mary Emmerling

text by Jill Kirchner Simpson

photographs by Carter Berg

Clarkson Potter/Publishers
New York

Published in the United States by Clarkson Potter/Publishers,
an imprint of the Crown Publishing Group,
a division of Random House, Inc., New York.
www.crownpublishing.com
www.clarksonpotter.com

Library of Congress Cataloging-in-Publication Data
Emmerling, Mary Ellisor.
Mary Emmerling's beach cottages : at home by the sea /
Mary Emmerling ; text by Jill Kirchner Simpson ; photographs
by Carter Berg. — 1st ed.
1. Cottages—Decoration—United States. 2. Vacation
homes—United States. 3. Seaside architecture—United
States. I. Kirchner, Jill. II. Berg, Carter. III. Title.
IV. Title: Beach cottages.
NK2195.C67E46 2008
747'.8872—dc22 2007033102

ISBN 978-0-307-33822-8

Printed in China

Photographs by Carter Berg

Design by Vanessa Holden

10 9 8 7 6 5 4 3 2 1

First Edition

REG — you are my support, my everything

SAMANTHA AND SAM, JONATHAN AND BETSEY—

for all your beach memories and sunsets

TERRY— for all those nights looking at the sunsets and stars with a glass of champagne—thanks, Brother

CONTENTS

If you grow up going to the ocean, you'll probably always be an ocean person. When you have many childhood memories of the beach, it becomes a part of you. My heart and my thoughts

are always at the beach, because I grew up spending summers in Rehoboth Beach, Delaware, and for several years even lived there year-round. I've always loved the view, the sound, the scent of the ocean. Whether it's sunny or stormy, foggy or cool and clear, the beach is simply a magical place.

So many of my favorite memories center on the beach—the warm sand under my feet, ocean swimming lessons from the lifeguards, those same lifeguards saving me in a riptide, finding money under the boardwalk (I made more money that way than babysitting for fifty cents an hour!), the jukeboxes and the amusement-park rides on the boardwalk, and collecting beachcombing

discoveries in a hanging shoe bag on the back of my closet door. My best friend's father owned the Dairy Queen, and he let us pretend we worked there on hot summer days. I learned to love vanilla Cokes at the local soda shop, with soda from the fountain (very important), and french fries with vinegar at Thrasher's on the boardwalk. Boy, did we have fun and adventures every single day! I still love a big summer rainstorm, nights cool enough for a fire in the fireplace, and the scent of pine trees at the beach in Henlopen.

When I was living in New York, I discovered the beautiful white sand beaches of the Hamptons, where I lived in various vacation cottages over the course of thirty years. And through my travels, I've found seaside pleasures all over the world—from the crystalline turquoise waters of St. Barths; to my little conch cottage in

Key West; to sunsets over the ocean in Laguna Beach, California; to riding horses and watching fireworks on New Year's Eve on one of my all-time favorite beaches in Puerto Vallarta, Mexico.

My friends joke that I can't live anywhere for more than three or four years, that I have to move to a new place and a new kind of house to inspire each new book. Well, it's true that not too long ago, my husband, Reg, and I started renting a little beach cottage in Laguna Beach, California, and now I am a convert to the pleasures of West Coast beach life. People love the beach here, and they know how to have fun! Though Reg and I have to travel a long distance to get there, once we arrive, it all seems worth it.

I guess I shouldn't be surprised that I have passed on my love of the beach to my children. My daughter, Samantha, married her husband, Sam Henning, at her father's beach house in Cape Cod; and my son, Jonathan, married his wife, Betsey McCall, in Key West, Florida. We have always loved the ocean, the sand, the sunsets. We always keep swimsuits and towels in the back of the car, ready for any adventure.

A beach house is meant to hold family and friends, memories and desires, joy and love, all within its simple walls. If you have ever loved a beach house, you know it holds a place in your heart forever.

Mary Emmerling

There is an implicit promise of freedom, a sense of escape and pure relaxation, embodied in the idea of a beach house. Henry James once famously called the words *summer afternoon*

"the two most beautiful words in the English language." For those fortunate enough to own homes by the sea, or live in them for an enchanted week or two each summer, the words *beach house* have the same evocative associations—life removed from pressures, schedules, work and school, the mundane concerns of everyday life. We leave those cares behind at our year-round homes, shed them like layers of winter clothing as we take that much-anticipated drive or ferry ride to some individual version of paradise.

Almost by definition, a beach house should reflect a simpler way of life, a pared-down existence where the

breeze is the housekeeper and a whisk of the broom across sandy floorboards might be the only work that gets done most days. A beach house should not be precious, or fragile, or impeccably neat. It prefers slipcovers and fabrics and furnishings that don't mind a damp swimsuit, the bleaching of the sun, or the grit of sand. Its treasures have often been culled freely from the coast—seashells, starfish, bits of driftwood and sea glass, flotsam and jetsam that count for jewels in this setting. The beach house's palette often reflects its surroundings as well—in hues of sea and sky, sailcloth and dune grass—paled by the sun and tumbled by the ocean. The beach house welcomes improvisation and accepts imperfections. A blanket serves as a headboard, a bedspread as a slipcover, a nautical chart or dog-eared photographs as art. Tag-sale finds and family castoffs make worthy furnishings; a coat of white paint unites mismatched eras and styles. The beach has a visual vocabulary, though the mainland often borrows from it, of wicker and canvas, director's chairs and chaise lounges, hammocks and awnings, slipcovers and straw rugs . . .

nothing that can't be renewed with a washing machine, a good hosing, or another coat of paint.

This simplicity is apparent in our back-to-basics approach to life at the beach, too. Clothes are fewer, meals less formal, the pace slower, the house only part-time—a retreat on rainy days or at night when tired, tanned, salty bodies tumble home from the outdoor playground of the shore. Then the glow of an oil lantern or citronella candles beckons from the porch, drawing family members home like moths. Time to rejuvenate with an outdoor shower, grab a drink, and settle in for a meal of fresh tomatoes and farmstand corn, the fisherman's catch, and a cooling finish of ice cream or juicy blueberries. Generations gather around the Monopoly or Scrabble board or play endless hands of Hearts for entertainment. Memories are inscribed at the beach, not necessarily of "big" moments or special occasions but rather pure, primal recollections of the scent of salt air or the warmth of the sun, the giddy thrill of fireworks or a roller coaster, the warm embrace of a grandparent's lap, the sparkle of the sun on the waves, the quiet solitude on the beach at the end of the day once everyone else has packed up and gone home.

The beach house is our tiny foothold in a place that can't really be captured or owned by any one person—the shoreline, the shifting sands, the dunes, the limitless horizon, an endless stretch of sea and sky. The beach's pleasures are pure, sensual ones—the danger and thrill of watching a storm advance across the sea, or of riding waves into the shore; of feeling the sun bathe one's whole body in warmth; of lying almost perfectly still while the mind empties out its cares like so many grains of sand.

While there are certainly beach houses that are quite grand and furnished as lavishly as any inland manse (particularly in communities like the Hamptons, Nantucket, and Malibu, which have grown incredibly expensive in recent years), the homes I want to share with you in this book fit my definition of "beach house style": They all reflect a connection to the place where they are situated and the more carefree lifestyle they are meant to encourage. While my own approach to decorating has always been rooted in the unpretentious charms of country style, the beach houses that appeal to me range from modern houses and interiors to more classic, traditional designs. They may be large

or small, old or new, on or near the water, but all of them show an appreciation for the idea of a beach house as a return to a simpler Eden—a place to pare down material possessions, maintenance, and fuss, and to get at the core of what we love and know to be most important in our lives: the chance to live more connected to nature, to share luxurious stretches of unscheduled and unpressured time with family and friends, and to tune out the din of everyday life in order to hear our own true inner voice again. Each of the home owners whose stories you will read here revels in the opportunity to live near the ocean, and the natural surroundings and more relaxed way of life influence their décor in creative and often unexpected ways.

Whether you own a beach house, rent one for a week each summer, or just live the fantasy in your mind, the beach house way of life is one that can appeal to and offer ideas to all of us. By reading the stories that follow, I hope you will glean lots of decorating inspiration, to be sure, but I also hope you will find beautiful, compelling incentives to live a simpler, less precious, and more enjoyable life all year long.

back to the basics

the beach girl

MARY EMMERLING ❧ LAGUNA BEACH, CALIFORNIA

I had a beach house in the Hamptons for years, another in Key West for a while, and I've visited many, many other beaches, but I had never lived in California before. Considering I have owned twenty-two different houses, this may be kind of surprising. Every time I went to Laguna Beach for a magazine shoot, I just had the feeling I should be living there. But because my job with *Country Home* magazine is based in Des Moines, Iowa; my husband, Reg, lives and works in Scottsdale, Arizona (where we also have a small house); and I am constantly on the road for work, southern California was not an obvious choice for a vacation house. And yet, Laguna Beach is close to a major airport, and . . . it *is* the beach! Finally, I couldn't resist.

Unfortunately, in the years since I had first contemplated buying a home in Laguna, about an hour south of Los Angeles, real estate prices there had skyrocketed. The beach shacks that once seemed pricey enough at $250,000 were now selling for $2 million! So two years ago Reg and I decided to rent something small but well situated. The house is just a tiny 600-square-foot bungalow built in the 1950s, but the minute

PREVIOUS PAGE ❧ On the front porch, lacy wicker chairs—unexpected in black—provide the "punctuation"; red-white-and-blue beach balls provide the fun.
LEFT ❧ White-slipcovered upholstery (with a matelassé spread for Cinco, our dog) and sisal rugs are naturals at the beach; taupe walls set off the white furnishings. I found the sailfish in New York, oddly enough, and had it shipped out here.
ABOVE ❧ Our simple 1950s beach shack is dressed up a bit by its distinctive porch railing. The front porch is the one we use in the morning, where we sip coffee and read the paper in the early sun.

I saw the view, I said, "I'll take it." It has front and back porches, with ocean views from both. We are about ten houses from the beach, and what I like about Laguna is that the houses are on a hillside, which is graduated to share the views. When houses are renovated or built new, they are not permitted to obstruct their neighbors' views.

What I also love about California is that it really has a sense of fun. It's beachy! Kids here go to school with a book bag over one arm and a surfboard under the other. California still seems to have that sense of freedom and adventure that has faded away in many other places. Every day is just another perfect day in

paradise. Of course, there is a rainy season, but most of the year the weather is gorgeous. And there is something about palm trees that says "instant vacation."

The house has two bedrooms and only one bathroom, but it's just big enough that we can fit in the kids when they come to visit. It was unfurnished, with a white kitchen, wood floors, a fireplace (wonderful because the evenings get cool on the ocean), and just a nice, simple white background that made it easy to move in. I brought pieces I had in storage from past houses in the Hamptons, Santa Fe, and even Key West, and I bought some new pieces, like the raffia sofa, which is the most comfortable one I've ever had. To complete the picture, I relied on my old faithfuls—white slipcovers, black-bordered sisal rugs, simple matchstick blinds, and white linen curtains blowing in the breeze. I prefer sisal or straw mats or bare floors in a beach house because of the sand, and I don't like to have drapes or anything heavy obscuring

ABOVE ❧ Tablescaping goes to the beach, with mercury glass compotes filled with shells topping stacks of art and design books. Binoculars, candles, and an ironstone pitcher filled with flowering and fruited branches complete the composition.

OPPOSITE ❧ A Santa Fe artisan made the driftwood mirror (as well as the child's chair on the deck, pictured on page 29).

the windows. Like nearly everyone who has a beach house, before I knew it I was buying paintings of the ocean and collecting seashells and sand dollars.

You have to have a sense of fun at the beach, or else you've lost all connection to your childhood. That's why I hung beaded curtains in the doorways (you can see out to the ocean, but the neighbors can't see in), a big sailfish over the sofa, and even a disco ball on the front porch! We keep fun, cheap plastic beach balls on the porch, too. By tossing one to kids walking by, we start up a conversation and meet the neighbors!

I also make sure to have plenty of sarongs, flip-flops and straw slippers, straw hats, and beach totes and towels on hand for guests. Peg racks, baskets, and shelves provide my favorite out-in-the-open storage. I love that we just get up in the morning and put on a swimsuit or shorts; you never really have to get dressed up at the beach.

People forget how wonderful it is to have a fireplace at the beach, where the nights often get chilly, especially early and late in the season. I found the gorgeous candelabra dripping with light-catching crystals at the Heart of Country antiques show in Nashville. Scatterings of starfish, sand dollars, and shells provide a fitting base for a painting of the ocean I picked up at an antiques mall.

Most of the time, we eat outside; if the weather doesn't cooperate, we eat in front of the fire on the tiny cocktail table. I have a larger table in the living room, but it got co-opted by piles of books, bowls of shells, candles, and all my other favorite finds. I've always preferred to see and enjoy my things rather than store and hide them away. And at the beach, keeping them in plain sight serves as a sort of three-dimensional memory book.

The bedrooms are simple: I use all-white linens, and then add color with a serape or a vstriped dhurrie. The headboard in our bedroom is actually an antique French mirror I bought years ago at a Bloomingdale's model room sale, turned sideways. It hung in the living room in my Santa Fe house, but when you move from place to place, you have to be inventive. In that same spirit, a striped dhurrie serves as a headboard of sorts in the compact guest room.

On both the front and back porches, I used black wicker furniture. I like to say that black is mascara for a house: It gives things a sharpness, an outline, and a focus. When everything is white and floating, the punctuation of black is necessary to ground it.

I'm always happy at the beach. There's no way you can be in a bad mood here, whether you're walking, biking, or just relaxing. I can have the worst plane ride getting here, or awful traffic, and the minute I walk in this house, I forget it all. I've made it.

ABOVE ✑ I don't think there's a house I've owned (or rented) that hasn't had at least one peg rack in it. This one holds straw hats, baseball caps, and cover-ups for the beach, adding storage in a small space while creating an engaging display.

OPPOSITE ✑ A simple white kitchen is all I require. If I stand on my tiptoes, I can see the ocean from the windows above the sink.

LEFT ❧ An antique French mirror turned on its side became our headboard. The glitter-dusted incantation to dream is by a California artist. A Mexican serape adds a bit of color to the white bed linens. The door, screened by an inexpensive beaded curtain, opens onto the back deck.

ABOVE ❧ I bought this painting in Mexico—it perfectly captures the poses of girls at the beach. A 1920s blue glass lamp echoes their curves. The shell cross is the beach variation of my large collection of crosses.

ABOVE ❧ Beaded curtains are like wind chimes that tinkle in the breeze, a vestige of the hippie era, when many of these beach houses were built. Palm trees and a sacred heart offer a little privacy as well as a shot of fun.
OPPOSITE ❧ The view from the front porch, in a word: sublime.

SOUNDS OF SUMMER

Anything by the four artists below is a summer classic.
Here are some good compilations of their songs:

Sounds of Summer: The Very Best of the Beach Boys
Legend: The Best of Bob Marley and the Wailers
*Songs You Know by Heart:
Jimmy Buffett's Greatest Hits*
The Best of Van Morrison

PLAYLIST

"Good Vibrations," the Beach Boys
"(Sittin' On) The Dock of the Bay," Otis Redding
"Walking on Sunshine," Katrina and the Waves
"Soak Up the Sun," Sheryl Crow
"Hot Fun in the Summertime,"
Sly and the Family Stone
"Dancing in the Street," Martha Reeves
and the Vandellas
"All Summer Long," the Beach Boys
"Margaritaville," Jimmy Buffett
"Under the Boardwalk," the Drifters
"Groovin'," the Young Rascals
"California Girls," the Beach Boys
"Hawaii Five-O," the Ventures
"In the Summertime," Mungo Jerry
"I Can See Clearly Now," Johnny Nash
"Good Day Sunshine," the Beatles
"Sail On, Sailor," the Beach Boys
"Three Little Birds," Bob Marley and the Wailers
"The Tide Is High," Blondie

the flip-flop life

LYNN SHERMAN AND LEONARD REISS ✺ KEY WEST, FLORIDA

Tucked away behind large Eureka palms and lush tropical foliage, this little Key West conch cottage feels private and secluded, even though it sits close to its neighbors. It's just a few blocks to the water, but what Lynn Sherman and her husband, Leonard Reiss, wanted most was to be in the old part of Key West, "with picket fences, old houses, next-door neighbors, and windy roads," says Lynn. "Judy Blume once said that Key West isn't Florida; it's an island in the Caribbean."

Lynn and her husband had been living in New York City, but after Leonard retired, they were ready for a change. "We wanted to find the equivalent of Greenwich Village in a warm place—you know the Woody Allen line

about needing to live somewhere where you can always walk home and get a sweater?" They visited Savannah, Sanibel Island, and Naples, Florida, but nothing grabbed them. "Key West came the closest," says Lynn, "but it didn't really win us over until we stayed there with friends and went to an AIDS benefit. We liked the diversity of people, of ages, of economic and

PREVIOUS PAGE ✏ Lynn converted the small one-car garage into a light-filled painting studio. "It's like a doll-house, but that's okay because I work small," says Lynn. Her pieces are shown at the Lucky Street Gallery in Key West.
ABOVE ✏ The artist at work painting her canvases, often portraits of houses or people that interest her.
RIGHT ✏ A long gallery runs along one side of the house, accessed by French doors, which shelters an outdoor dining table as well as wicker seating.

geographic backgrounds, and we loved the sense of community. It is a warm, giving community where it's easy to meet people."

Lynn and Leonard rented for a month one winter, then started looking around to rent for longer or buy. "When I walked into this house, I said, 'This is it,'" she remembers. "This" was a hundred-year-old cottage that had been subtly updated by Boston architect Charles Meyer, son-in-law of the previous owners. You enter into a long hall paneled with the indigenous Dade County pine, with a small guest room and study off to the side, "Then, 'ta-da,' you walk into a bright white room with twenty-five-foot-high ceilings," says Lynn. That one big, open room is an easygoing home to living room, dining area, and kitchen, and offers a view of the lap pool outside, its turquoise brilliance reflected on the white plank ceiling. French doors open to a porch

running along the side of the house with its own small dining table. "You can sit out there and listen to the wonderful sound of the rain on the tin roof," says Lynn. There are no screens, but miraculously "there are no mosquitoes." The master bedroom and bath are tucked into an upstairs loft space.

Lynn is an artist, and she was drawn to the light in Key West. "I felt like I could paint here forever—it's

OPPOSITE ⤶ Notes Lynn, "I can't resist a surface; I'm always making little tablescapes from things I love," like this arrangement on a Chinese table in the living room.
ABOVE ⤶ The great room is the heart of Lynn's home, the "ta-da" room, as she calls it, with 25-foot-high ceilings, white-slipcovered furniture, and wraparound windows opening onto views of lush tropical foliage and a lap pool.

like the light artists talk about in Provence or the Hamptons." She hired Charles Meyer to knock down the one-car garage and convert it into a studio for her. "We had to keep it the same size, so it's like a dollhouse, but my paintings are usually only nine by twelve inches, so it works fine for me," she says.

In a previous life, Lynn was an interior designer in Philadelphia. "I was the queen of white," she says. "All

my life, I've had white walls, white sheets, white everything. If people didn't like white, they didn't hire me." Here, she took her cues from the existing house and kept the floors and some of the furnishings dark, "more like a British Colonial house in the islands," but her trademark white cotton slipcovers still keep the feeling airy and light. "I like for the paintings and the people to be the color," she says. Even her garden has white flowers only. A long wall of shelves and cabinets showcases artwork, books, and accessories.

In the summer, Lynn and Leonard head north to a home in Harvey Cedars, on Long Beach Island in New Jersey, where Lynn has been going her whole life. There, they live a quieter, more family-centered version of the beach life. The best part, says Lynn, is that "we wear the same clothes all year round now. I don't really have shoes anymore, just flip-flops. It's very freeing."

ABOVE ← A row of bookshelves and cabinets lines one wall of the great room; in the kitchen they become shelving for dishes and glasses. Baskets provide a textural crown.
OPPOSITE ← The airy white master bedroom tucked into the second floor "feels garret-like," says Lynn. Closets and cabinets are tucked into the eaves. Louvered wood shutters and a ceiling fan keep the breezes blowing.

ABOVE ❧ "I never liked orchids before I moved here," says Lynn. "Now I buy them regularly—only white ones, though." Her garden has only white flowers.

OPPOSITE ❧ A long, narrow lap pool surrounded by palms creates a lush, refreshing interlude in the tiny backyard, visible from the living room and master bedroom.

key west's conch cottages

What is a conch house, anyway? And where did it get its name?

Early settlers in the Bahamas and the Florida Keys did not have bricks or stone, but created mortar for their homes using sand, water, and lime. They made the lime by burning conch shells, which were once abundant on the islands. Thus the term *conch house* was born, though it also came to describe the small clapboard cottages built by ship's carpenters and settlers. These cottages have multi-cultural roots that draw on building forms from both the Caribbean and the New England seacoast. Many have standing-seam metal roofs to reflect the heat of the sun, deep porches or verandas, and louvered shutters to block the afternoon sun while allowing the breeze to flow. They are often built on piers in case of flooding and to allow air to circulate and cool the house.

Conch is also often used to refer to natives or lifelong residents of the Florida Keys and the Bahamas, and it is a term of honor, not derision. In the past, parents placed a conch shell on a stick in front of the house to announce the birth of a child. Newcomers are sometimes referred to as *freshwater conches*, and people active in the community are dubbed *honorary conches*.

oh, galveston

SHIRLEY AND KIRBY FORTENBERRY   GALVESTON, TEXAS

Galveston Island, Texas, was a prosperous port city
in the mid to late 1800s, lined with beautiful Victorian houses.
Then the Great Storm of 1900, the deadliest natural disaster in U.S. history,
wiped out much of the island. "Across the street from our house, a hundred people miraculously survived the storm
huddled on the third floor," says Shirley Fortenberry, who has been going to Gulf Coast beaches all her life. "There
are plaques on houses that say 'Survived the Storm.'" But Galveston never quite recovered. A channel was dug
inland to Houston, which became the main port and thriving metropolis of young Texas.

    In some ways, that turn of events was for the best, because Galveston, a narrow, 32-mile-long island reached

by bridge from the mainland, is once again thriving, but now as a vacation and tourist destination. After the hurricane, a large seawall was built to protect the island from storms in the Gulf of Mexico. The beach sits behind it, and you can drive along the coast on top of the seawall. The city now has four historic preservation districts with a well-endowed historical foundation,

PREVIOUS PAGE A bamboo cabinet showcases coral in the front entry. The worn, painted pine chest it sits on echoes the pine woodwork throughout the house.
LEFT In the living room, a sophisticated neutral palette of mushroom-colored walls ("Flax" from Sherwin-Williams) and linen-covered furnishings accomplished Shirley's goal of a "calm and restful" home.
ABOVE The Fortenberrys' 1911 home boasts porches on both levels, typical of Victorian homes in the area.

and many of the ornate old Victorians have been rebuilt and restored.

The opportunity to save and preserve an old home drew the Fortenberrys to Galveston (their year-round home is an old log house in Texas hill country). "We don't have a lot of old homes here in Texas. That's what I love about Galveston—there are so many people here trying to preserve the architecture," says Shirley. "Our house is a fairly simple house, built in 1911 after the

storm. It's constructed of pine and cypress, and thanks to the invention of balloon construction, it gives in the wind, so it survived the 1913 storm."

Because Galveston has been a port and a military town, many of the houses were divided into multiple dwellings during economic downturns. When Shirley and her husband, Kirby, bought the house in 2001, it was divided into rooms for an owner and two tenants. "Someone lived where the dining room and kitchen are, and renters lived in the upstairs bedrooms. It was still in good shape structurally, but we had to take out some walls and put it back together." The Fortenberrys removed an old coal-burning stove that ran from the first to the second floor and repurposed its brick for a courtyard around the house. They ripped out Sheetrock and a fake fireplace that had been added, and installed central heat and air, though they use air-conditioning only in the hottest part of summer. "These

ABOVE ❧ A master at reinvention, Shirley painted zebra stripes on straw place mats to camouflage stains. The antique oval plates are perfect for lobster.
OPPOSITE ❧ The dining room chandelier came from an old theater in Galveston; the beads are left over from Mardi Gras. Shirley had the narrow console table built to fit between the two windows and draped it in linen.

older homes were built to take in the prevailing south-easterly wind," explains Shirley, so they often open the windows, doors, and transoms and just let the breeze blow through the house, keeping it comfortably cool.

Like many Galveston homes, this house has two front porches, one on each floor, another naturally cooling architectural feature. "One reason I love the old homes is that they all have porches where you can catch the breeze," says Shirley. "People sit outside or walk around and talk to their neighbors. Porches create great neighborhoods where people really know each other."

Kirby walks along the beach every morning; Shirley loves to fish off its jetties and piers, often catching speckled trout, flounder, and redfish. "You can catch your dinner, or you can walk over to the bay, where all the shrimp boats come in, and buy fresh shrimp, oysters, lobster, crab, and flounder right off the boat. And there are so many great restaurants here, you don't have to

cook at all!" Though they come to Galveston all year round, they like spring and fall the best, when it's less crowded with tourists. "We have 'Dickens on the Strand' at Christmastime, and Mardi Gras is a huge event here in February, as is the house tour the first of May."

Shirley has a good eye and familiarity with design, having worked for a decorator in Houston and as an illustrator for NASA, as well as in advertising and

OPPOSITE ← Prints of fish and, on another wall, seashells, subtly hint at the home's seaside location; the starfish artfully propped against the set of books further underscores it in this charming vignette in the living room.
ABOVE ← An old French cupboard with distinctive glass-front doors in the living room displays coral and shells among its books.

real estate. When it came time to decorate their beach house, Shirley wanted to simplify the house and eliminate some of its excesses, like the faux-painted black rope trim in the downstairs bath, as well as a faux-painted cloud ceiling. "It was a little too over-the-top for me," says Shirley. She chose a deep flax color for the downstairs walls to form a rich, neutral backdrop for furnishings slipcovered in natural linen. The original pine

ABOVE ⮜ Shirley painted the diamonds on the old wood floors of the powder room using porch paint.
OPPOSITE ⮜ Shirley and Kirby remade the kitchen from the old kitchen and porch, matching new bead-board walls to the original ceiling. Simple cabinets and butcher block countertops gain warmth and personality from still life paintings of food that Shirley has collected.

floors wear simple sea-grass rugs, and inexpensive matchstick blinds hang on the windows.

"I love old painted pieces, but they're getting harder to find," she says, so in many places she used pine furniture, which matches the original floors, woodwork, and staircase. "A lot of the older homes here are very Victorian, with mahogany furniture that is heavy and ornate. I wanted something old, soft, and informal, like pine." A diamond-paned glass-front cabinet that was wrong in yellow works perfectly painted white and filled with an engaging mix of antique books, transferware platters, coral, and shells. Old engravings of seashells and fish on the walls add to the beachy feeling.

Shirley painted the floor of the bathroom herself in a diamond pattern. "It reads 'country,' but the Galveston sidewalks were actually once a very sophisticated diamond-patterned slate. The porch across the street once had a diamond floor of marble. I was going to paint my porch floor as well, but then I ran out of steam," she confesses. "I said, 'Let's have a party instead!'" The original bath had bead-board walls, so when they turned the old porch into a kitchen, they chose bead board for its walls, with simple white-painted cabinets and butcher-block counters.

"When I first started the house, I remembered Mary Emmerling's advice I had once read, which was to take notes about your goals and what you wanted your house to be," says Shirley. "The goal I wrote down was that I wanted the house to feel restful and calm, very livable, with no superfluous detail. Now people always come in and say what a peaceful house this is, so I feel like I achieved my goal."

ABOVE ❧ Shirley covered the headboard and made the bed skirt and curtains all with burlap costing just $2 a yard. They wrap the master bedroom in the softness of fabric, layered with the pronounced texture of burlap. She opted for the honeyed warmth of antique pine furniture.
OPPOSITE ❧ A handsome pond yacht is perhaps the quintessential beach house accessory.

four to one

SAGAPONACK, NEW YORK

For many years, I owned a quartet of little cottages in the Hamptons on Long Island. (My longtime readers might remember them from *Mary Emmerling's American Country Cottages* or from one of the magazine stories they appeared in.) This set of small shingled fisherman's cottages built in the 1960s—two studio and two two-bedroom cottages—was nestled in the dunes in a captivating oceanside setting in Sagaponack.

Despite the coveted location of the cottages, no one could quite figure out what to do with their unconventional configuration. I decided to preserve them as much as possible, keeping their shingled exteriors, fieldstone fireplaces, and original details—while making them white, light, and airy inside. I moved into one two-bedroom

cottage, and my teenage children and guests stayed in the other cottages. Each one was decorated differently—a sort of "greatest hits" of my favorite country styles, from the western-themed "Stars" to the romantic vintage florals of "True Love."

When I decided to move to Santa Fe ten years ago, I put my beloved cottages on the market, but once again, potential buyers weren't exactly sure what to do with them. A young family in New York had been rent-

PREVIOUS PAGE ✐ The architect linked two of the original cottages with a two-story addition in the center, which houses the living room, and upstairs, the master bedroom suite. A screened porch was added as well.
ABOVE ✐ One of the original cottages was preserved as a guesthouse.
LEFT ✐ The eat-in kitchen was created from one of the original studio cottages. Open shelving and an old farmhouse table serving as an island create a relaxed country feel.

ing the main cottage from me in the off-season. "One day I was up on a stepladder replacing the bulb in a spotlight when I realized I had a hundred-eighty-degree view of the ocean from up there," my renter, John, told me, "and I thought, If the cottage had a second story, it would have amazing oceanfront views." He set about investigating the possibility of combining the cottages while preserving their original charm and detail. Working with a talented local architect, Katherine McCoy; the builder who had originally renovated the cottages for me, Greg Peterson; and a local lawyer, John was

able to navigate the complex zoning and building restrictions on the property and come up with a plan to integrate the cottages into a single-family home. As part of the agreement to build the house, one cottage was relocated to Wainscott. They kept the studio cottage as a guesthouse, and then McCoy cleverly joined the two remaining cottages with a central connecting piece, which consists of a living room and a dining room, with a master bedroom suite, a study, and a small porch on a new second floor. And as John had envisioned up on that stepladder, "When we're lying in bed we have a wonderful unobstructed view of the ocean."

"We wanted to preserve the look and feel of the original fishing cottages as much as possible," says John, "because that's what we fell in love with." To that end, they matched the original door and window casings and floorboards, and repurposed everything they could from the original structures. "Many of the furnishings

ABOVE ✦ The second-story master bedroom has a generous window seat from which to take in the ocean views. Exposed rafters give the room an open feel. Simple canvas curtain panels are hung from hooks and grommets.
OPPOSITE ✦ Antique wicker with vintage floral pillows offers cozy seating on the screened porch. Doors open onto the lawn and pool.

became a bedroom suite for the couple's two daughters, ages nine and thirteen, incorporating a playroom and a bedroom for their son, age six. The studio cottage, on the other side, became an eat-in kitchen. A small gunite pool surrounded by bluestone and a screened porch further enhance the family's enjoyment of outdoor living. And on cooler nights, there are five fireplaces, including the guest cottage's, to keep things warm and cozy.

"As soon as school ends, my wife and the children move out to the beach for the entire summer. But even in the off-season, no one ever turns down a chance to go out there," he says. For city kids who spend the rest of the year in a sea of concrete in Manhattan, "they get a chance to live barefoot. They're at the beach every day."

The renovation and addition also offered the opportunity to install new wiring, high-speed Internet, and other modern luxuries such as air-conditioning, "but when you're that close to the ocean, you only turn on the AC five days a year," says John. "There are also no bugs. The doors stay open all summer." He proudly muses, "There's no more beautiful beach on earth than the Hamptons in July and August. It's the only place I've seen where you can have fields of corn right up to the sand dunes and ocean. In the summer, the hydrangeas and roses here are unbelievable, yet you're so close to the ocean you can hear it, smell it, and see it. There are very few houses left like this anymore. It's truly something special."

OPPOSITE ✎ The girls and their golden retriever play in the ocean, just steps from the house.
ABOVE ✎ Grab-and-go storage: A parade of colorful swimsuits hangs from a peg rack in the girls' bedroom suite.

keep it simple

Ginger Barber has been going to Galveston as long as she's lived in Texas, nearly thirty years now. "It's only forty-five minutes to an hour from Houston to Galveston, so it's easy to get there for weekends," she explains. "But once I arrive, I feel like I'm worlds away." Time slows down, she puts the car keys aside, and the fastest mode of transportation might be a golf cart or a surfboard. She exchanges the harried pace of the city for quiet mornings on the porch listening to the birds in the sanctuary across the way and calm evenings watching the sun slip behind the horizon at the end of the day.

For many years, Ginger rented homes near the beach, until finally one day she started exploring buying a place.

She came across an unfinished town house that over-looks the bay on the west end of Galveston. "It's on a little peninsula. You can see the bay out the front and the beach and ocean across a field out the back door." A single mother, Ginger felt it would be an ideal place to spend time with her fifteen-year-old son. "I have only a

PREVIOUS PAGE ✜ A lighthouse fashioned from twigs, old wood, buoys, and a birdcage form an evocative vignette on the porch.
LEFT ✜ Ginger removed the upper cabinet doors to create informal open shelving in the kitchen. An island custom-made from old wood wraps around the range.
ABOVE LEFT ✜ Bookshelves are filled with coral and shells Ginger has collected on her travels.
ABOVE RIGHT ✜ Ginger and her dog love walks by the ocean.

few more years before he leaves for college," she says wistfully. There's plenty for him and his friends to do—head to the beach, the pool, or the golf course, go surfing or Jet Skiing—and plenty for Ginger not to do, leaving her time to enjoy quieter endeavors such as bird-watching, kayaking, cooking, and beachcombing.

Though Ginger is a successful interior designer in Houston, here at the beach, she wanted nothing more than to stick to the basics: "I wanted this place to be family-friendly—slipcovers, sea-grass rugs, seashells, wicker, and pine. Keeping it simple makes it feel like you're at a beach house—you know you've left the city." The house is a manageable 1,500 square feet, and it doesn't have a big yard, so Ginger can "just lock up and go at the end of the weekend."

To furnish the house, Ginger found old pine pieces and had them stripped, bleached, or whitewashed to give them the feel of weathered driftwood. Ginger chose everything for comfort and ease: In the living room, the strong texture of a wicker hassock grounds the comfy white canvas and natural linen–covered upholstery. She picks up pieces of antique green wicker as she comes across them for a splash of color and texture. An old dining table, stripped of its dark finish, has the feel of a stylish picnic table. It is surrounded by informal director's chairs, which can be easily folded and taken outside, and spiffed up with a wash of their canvas covers. "There's not much art on the walls," says Ginger—schoolroom charts of botanicals, shell engravings, simple prints. She lined the narrow bookshelves in the hall not with china or precious antiques but rather with shells she's collected from travels to Costa Rica and elsewhere.

"Where we really live is the screened porch, which runs along the living and dining room on the side of the

ABOVE ✺ Washable linen and cotton canvas slipcovers create dressed-down ease in the living room. An antique school chart serves as large-scale botanical art.
OPPOSITE ✺ Ginger stripped a dark dining table to reveal the wood grain, and conversely darkened the wood frames of the director's chairs to make them look richer.

house," says Ginger. "It's like an extension of my living room. And there's always a breeze by the bay." With wicker furniture gathered around a tall coffee table, it can easily serve for outdoor dining, or as the perfect place for summer reading or dozing.

In the kitchen, Ginger took all the doors off the upper cabinets and filled the shelves with her dishes and glassware for a more cottagey feel. She had an island custom made from old wood that wraps around the gas stove, and she placed an open shelf underneath for baskets and large pots.

In the end, what draws her to this home and to Galveston isn't so much the décor, it's having a place to be with family and friends, enjoy the outdoors, and simply relax.

LEFT 🍃 White and leafy linens in the master bedroom contrast with the rugged texture of sea-grass rugs and baskets. Worn painted furniture and lamps made from old balusters add the appealing patina of age to a new house.
ABOVE 🍃 A bamboo hall tree serves as an impromptu closet/display space.

vintage romance

miami nice

LIZ AND MICHAEL PIERCE ❧ MIAMI, FLORIDA

Liz and Michael Pierce live most of the year in New York, in a long, narrow loft buried in the gray canyons of downtown. But on vacations and long weekends, they escape to a different palette of sun-washed pinks, faded sky blues, and sunny lemon yellows in South Beach, Miami. Michael is an architect who, with partner DD Allen, divides his time between projects in Miami and New York. In the early 1990s, he purchased this 1923 stucco Mediterranean in somewhat run-down condition. The surrounding South Beach neighborhood, likewise, was a faded echo of a once-glamorous enclave of Mediterranean houses and Art Deco hotels. Since then, both the house and the area have enjoyed a dramatic refurbishing and resurgence.

Michael and Liz, a freelance art director and designer who's worked for clients such as Williams-Sonoma, Coach, and Pottery Barn, were married in 1994 and embarked on a renovation of the house as their time and budget allowed. "We took a lot of our wedding money and just started planting," says Liz. "There was nothing here, but everything grows so lushly that we now have palm trees and cascades of bougainvillea. A ficus hedge we planted for privacy is now twelve feet high, and it inspired everyone else on our block to start growing hedges as well, so the street is lined with walls of green." They replaced a small backyard with a shimmering cross-shaped pool of turquoise that reads "instant tropics."

Inside the house, Michael masterminded a judicious renovation, combining a closet-like kitchen and a dining room marred by a dropped ceiling and a lack of windows. He transformed the space into a wide galley kitchen with a pantry and a dining alcove with French doors that open to the terrace and pool. Michael maintained the Mediterranean spirit of the house by replicating the arched doorways used on the exterior and taking out some ill-advised "modernizations" like cabinets jury-rigged beneath the stairs.

Meanwhile, Liz worked her own tropical magic with color, paint, fabric, and tiles, pulling in finds from her

PREVIOUS PAGE ✒ Pareos, sarongs, and bathing suits create a colorful beach parade across hooks in the bedroom.

ABOVE ✒ In the "Florida room," a 1960s addition that opens to the pool, Liz installed black-and-white checkerboard cement tiles for cool-on-the-feet glamour. It's furnished with a casual assemblage of thrift-shop and estate-sale finds, like the $50 French settee and a white Barcalounger.

OPPOSITE ✒ In the entry hall, Liz outlined doorways and created moldings with gray-green paint. A painting from Mexico is "framed" in the same paint. Candleholders, sconces (now wired for electricity) and crosses, also bought in Mexico, mix with shells from Florida.

travels in Mexico as well as some impressive thrift-shop bargains, many picked up at the nearby Jewish Relief Center, like the French settee she unearthed for $50. She found inexpensive black-and-white cement tiles ($3 per square foot) similar to encaustic tiles she had seen in France and installed a classic checkerboard floor in the entry foyer and an adjacent Florida room that had been added in the 1960s. She had the tiles aged to look as though they'd always been there, and they evoke

LEFT ❧ Curvy vintage chairs in the living room are united with a French modern toile. Their sunny hue meets sky-colored stripes in a dhurrie rug.

ABOVE ❧ An arched alcove beneath the stairs has become a small shrine of sorts.

1920s Miami glamour while standing up well to sand and wet feet.

In the living room, the Pierces replaced an electric fireplace with an authentic wood-burning one and added a mantel. Liz slipcovered all the furniture in a graphic modern toile she'd bought in France and once envisioned making into bridesmaid dresses. "I'd always wanted to do all the pieces in a room in one fabric," says Liz, and here the crisp gold-and-white print unites a quartet of curvy 1940s flea-market chairs and a shapely chaise—a fresh alternative to the standard couch-and-two-chairs arrangement.

When they first moved in, Liz hated the "Pepto-Bismol pink" exterior, but she soon discovered what native Floridians know: that the sun quickly bleaches strong hues into soft pastels. The exterior is now a perfect shell pink, which she echoed in the master bedroom and guest bedroom. After experimenting with a variety of colors in the foyer, she decided that because each room affords a view of other rooms, it would be best to choose a unified palette downstairs. She chose Benjamin Moore's Dove White for walls and a gray-green (Horizon Gray) to create trompe l'oeil baseboards and surrounds for the arches. Upstairs, shades of pale icy blue and soft pink are quiet echoes of the vibrant flowers and water outside. "I wanted more muted, faded colors inside—they seemed to go with the beachy Mediterranean feel better," says Liz. She also liberally used her friend Mary Mulcahy's hand-blocked Indiennes fabrics,

ABOVE ✎ The vestibule once featured jury-built cabinets beneath the stairs; Michael restored the staircase to clean white plaster with a wrought-iron railing. A simple cloth-draped table serves as a hall bench.
OPPOSITE ✎ Michael, an architect, combined a tiny kitchen and dining room into a wide galley kitchen with a dining alcove. French doors by the table open to the outdoors.

LEFT ✦ The bedrooms are dressed in "Les Indiennes" hand-blocked linens. The paisley here, in the master bedroom, is set on an airy white ground for a more modern approach to classic Provençal patterns. A simple canopy made of fabric hung from a ring adds a touch of romance and camouflages the window behind the bed.

ABOVE ✦ Instead of a small, scraggly lawn, Michael designed a 40-foot-long cross-shaped pool edged in glass mosaic tiles for a resort-like backyard.

CHECKLIST FOR A
WELL-PACKED BEACH BAG

Pareo/sarong

Lightweight shirt

Sunscreen and lip sunblock

Beach towel or blanket

Flip-flops

Sunglasses

Straw hat or baseball cap

Hairbrush

Insect repellent

Wet wipes

iPod in protective case

Paperback novel

Baby powder (to help brush off sand)

Ziplock bags

Mini first-aid kit, including Benadryl and ibuprofen

Collapsible beach chair with carrying strap

Money and ID in waterproof wallet or pouch

Beach tag, if required

inspired by the fabrics of Provence, on bedding and daybeds, canopies, and throw pillows, to add a splash of color and pattern tempered by plenty of white.

For many years, Florida seemed as much a place to work as relax, as Liz and Michael invested lots of elbow grease in fixing up their home. "I don't like being in a place that looks ugly, so I wanted to get to the point where we could just enjoy it," says Liz. Now that they've finally reached that milestone, their Miami home is a place where they love to entertain, gather with friends, and enjoy the respite from New York's cold, gray winters. In the summer, it may be a little hot, but "it's nice because it's so uncrowded. When you're sitting out back, you don't even know there's another world outside," says Liz. "I'll often just go to the beach in the morning for a swim, pick up some ceviche, and then stay home. It's a perfect little oasis."

A fabric-covered screen, a table, a chair, and a mirror create an impromptu dressing room off the master bedroom. Liz added wood shutters throughout the house to help modulate the strong sun.

in black and white

Debbie and Rod Canada bought this cottage on the boardwalk in Newport Beach, California, eight years ago as a weekend getaway. It was only about an hour's drive from their inland home in Redlands, California—"but it was harder and harder for me to pull myself away from Newport Beach and head back home each weekend," says Debbie. After three years, when her youngest son left home for college, she and Rod decided to take the plunge and move to Newport Beach year-round. Even though her husband now commutes an hour and fifteen minutes each way to work, he says, "Once I cross over the bridge and see the water, it's worth it."

"When we were just coming here on weekends, I was playing around with how I wanted it to look, and it was

more casual," says Debbie, who has a passion for decorating, though she doesn't practice it professionally. "Then, when we sold our house in Redlands and were going to live here full-time, we really needed to make it a home." They redid the bathrooms and kitchen while preserving the original character and charm of the 1912 house as much as possible. They tore up the carpet and discovered wonderful old wood floors—"That made a huge difference," says Debbie—which they stripped of layers of paint and stained a dark umber. In the kitchen, they made significant changes without undergoing a

PREVIOUS PAGE ❧ Debbie's distinctive collection of bottle stoppers in the entry includes such shore-inspired elements as shells, coral, starfish, and a sea horse.
LEFT ❧ The ticking-stripe sofa in the living room kicked off the black-and-white scheme; piping from the same fabric outlines the white club chairs. The long window seat is one of the golden retrievers' favorite spots to lounge.
ABOVE ❧ Pink Iceberg roses climb the clapboard walls, adding cottage charm to the exterior.

full-scale renovation, refacing the cabinets and replacing the Formica counters with soapstone. The Canadas ripped up eight layers of linoleum, took out the fluorescent lighting, covered the exposed pipes with bead board, and added a pantry to the diminutive space. Debbie, opting to keep the vintage stove, had it reconditioned, rechromed, and reenameled at Antique Stove Heaven in Los Angeles. Elsewhere, the changes were largely cosmetic, though they replaced some modern windows in the master bedroom with old-fashioned double-hung windows to match the rest of the house.

The house is only about 2,200 square feet, but it boasts six bedrooms—two downstairs (one is used as a den) and four tucked under the eaves upstairs—so there's plenty of room for visiting family. One room even has a small sink and countertop that's a perfect changing station for Debbie's baby nephew.

Another guest bedroom houses an array of black-and-white photographs of old Newport Beach that Debbie found through a retired photographer and had enlarged and framed. They are the perfect embodiment of a house where nearly every room offers a simple, crisp study in black and white—not a common palette at the beach, but one that suits this turn-of-the-century house perfectly. "The house was gray when we bought it. We painted it white and added black shutters and awnings, and it just kind of snowballed from there," explains Debbie, who started with a black-and-white

ABOVE ✺ Built-in cupboards in the dining room, lined with black-and-white striped wallpaper, show off Debbie's collection of shapely white ironstone pitchers and platters. OPPOSITE ✺ Debbie and Rod made significant upgrades to the kitchen, refacing the cabinets, replacing Formica countertops with soapstone, and covering up exposed pipes with bead board. Debbie had the existing vintage stove reenameled and rechromed.

ticking-striped couch, then continued with everything from black wicker chairs and an iron bed to black-and-white striped wallpaper in the dining room. "I like black and white because it's a classic that will never go out of style," she adds. Now that her children are grown and she has trained her dogs not to jump up on the couches and beds unless they're covered with old quilts, Debbie finds it quite easy to live with white fabrics and linens at the beach, especially because they're all washable.

In the guest rooms, there are touches of dark brown and red, which add splashes of color while still comple-menting the carefully edited palette. Many of Debbie's

LEFT A mustard-colored bureau offers one of the few touches of color in the master bedroom, and indeed, the house. A wicker chair and trunk bestow texture.
ABOVE A black iron bed and dark matchstick blinds in the master bedroom contrast with the all-white bed linens, upholstery, and floaty curtains. The board-and-batten walls are all original to the house.

UNDER THE BOARDWALK

You can still find the old-fashioned pleasures of a boardwalk—Ferris wheels, surrey bikes, saltwater taffy— or just a beautiful place to stroll at these boardwalks:

Ocean City, Maryland

Rehoboth Beach, Delaware

Old Orchard Beach, Maine

Santa Cruz, California

Ocean City, New Jersey

Virginia Beach, Virginia

Venice Beach, California

Hollywood, Florida

Laguna Beach, California

Long Beach, Washington

Bethany Beach, Delaware

Mission Beach, California

favorite collectibles, from white ironstone and black-and-white seashell engravings to simple iron lanterns, effortlessly fall into line. Many of her finds also reflect the charmed seaside setting, such as the wood oars, some painted black, that Debbie cleverly hung in the narrow triangles formed by the eaves; the pressed fan coral framed in the guest room; and her treasured collection of handcrafted bottle stoppers, which includes seashells, starfish, and even a seahorse.

The Canadas' home fronts the beach and a cement boardwalk where people amble, bike, and run right by their front terrace. Their two golden retrievers love to perch on the window seats (with cushions covered in Sunbrella fabric to handle both the sun and the dogs) and watch the world go by. Debbie prefers the quieter pace of the off-season but savors the ocean views, the "incredible sunsets over Catalina Island," and the easy interaction with friends and neighbors. While they also loved their redwood-ringed home in Redlands, "It's just a whole different feel here," says Debbie. "It's so sunny and bright, it cheers me up just to be here."

The bedrooms are tucked under the eaves of the house's second floor. In this red and white guest room, an old oar fits perfectly on the sloping slice of wall.

the happy house

Rachel Ashwell, known around the world for her trademark Shabby Chic style, doesn't live in the crumbling old mansion you might expect. Though her last home in Malibu was from the 1920s, this one is all about location, location, location. Situated in the Malibu Colony, the exclusive street that hugs the Malibu coast, it was the first house she found in the neighborhood she loved, and she decided to take it.

A master of reinvention and seeing the best in the less than perfect, Rachel faced a true challenge this time: a musty, moldy 1950s ranch house. Wanting to make the most of her time with her teenage children, who were about to leave the nest, she decided to forgo a major renovation in favor of a few simple, big-payoff fix-ups like putting in

new windows, ripping out the shag carpeting and putting in cool limestone floors, and refurbishing the garden. She kept the basic U-shaped layout of the house intact and furnished it somewhat sparingly. "It's all about the views of the garden and the windows; it doesn't need a lot of decoration," says Rachel. There's not much art on the walls, and even fewer window treatments. "The light

PREVIOUS PAGE ✍ Rachel brought the home's lush gardens back to life.
LEFT ✍ In the family room, Rachel's signature slip-covered white sofas and chairs surround an embroidered white leather ottoman from Morocco she's employed as a soft, put-your-feet-up alternative to a coffee table. The all-white furnishings invite the view outdoors to be the focal point.
ABOVE ✍ Naturally iridescent shells gleam on a tiny outdoor table with an oxidized metal patina.

and the beach, and I didn't feel the need or desire to have two of everything, so I just split my belongings between the two houses," Rachel explains. "I guess I'm also going through the typical forties thing of wanting to simplify my life. I spent my twenties and thirties collecting, and now I'm thinking, 'What can I get rid of?'" she adds. "If this were an old cottage, it would need more fabrics, paintings, and so forth. But this house is breezy, sensual, and minimal, without compromising on comfort."

Slightly more tailored white sofas (still slipcovered), round white leather ottomans from Morocco, simple all-white bed linens, and a few pale colored pillows create a more streamlined look, though Rachel still remains true to her Shabby Chic roots. Her "forever" palette of faded pinks, turquoise, ivory, and white is "beach compatible," she points out. The worn and faded fabrics echo what the sun does naturally. And scattered about her house and patio are shells, sea glass, and old

in Malibu is so amazing, all you need is natural light by day and candlelight by night," she finds.

For the founder of Shabby Chic, who has espoused big, squishy slipcovered sofas, peeling painted furniture, old chandeliers dripping with crystals, and layers of faded floral patterns, the furnishings are surprisingly minimal. "I divide my time between 'town'—a house in Brentwood—

ABOVE ⮜ The frills and flounces of vintage prom dresses from the 1950s and '60s inspire Rachel to add a little whimsy to her designs and to her life.
OPPOSITE ⮜ Stacks of table linens line the shelves of a cupboard in the dining room. "Even at the beach, I like to use real cloth napkins," says Rachel. "They're not ironed or pristine, but they still make a meal feel a bit special."

dresses offers inspiration and whimsy. "Life can become rather staid," observes Rachel. "These are frivolous, and whether it's the detail of a ruffle or a fabric flower, they keep my eyes and my creativity open."

Like all beach homes, the emphasis here is on the outdoors: "The doors are rarely closed. There are lush gardens in front and back with fig, orange, and lemon trees; lavender; and an old rose garden." The property was once the garden for the beach house across the street, so it still has great soil, but she worked hard to refurbish it and give it a new lease on life.

"Having grown up in England not seeing much blue sky, I still find the clear, sunny skies and palm trees a novelty, even after twenty-five years," says Rachel. "It's been lovely for raising children—they barely even put on shoes until they were teenagers. And now that my kids are older and I'm traveling more, this is a wonderful low-maintenance house that's easy to live in. Everyone calls it 'the happy house.'"

tiled tables. "Wherever I am, I like the bohemian hippie thing, but with a dash of elegance," says Rachel. "White, turquoise, embroidery—they all feel like the sea to me." She painted the walls with white semigloss rather than matte paint, to suggest the feel of the cool white plaster walls in Greek island houses.

In this simple setting, small flourishes stand out: A garment rack in the living room filled with vintage prom

ABOVE ✢ Rachel kept her master bedroom as simple as possible. Even the oversize beveled mirror is propped casually against the wall.
OPPOSITE ✢ In the bath, a curvy antique mirror and sconces lend femininity to a white console sink; a painted dresser offers storage along with the appealing patina of age.

ABOVE ❧ A lacy white wrought-iron table and chairs provide outdoor eating beneath a shady canopy of trees.
BELOW ❧ Teak chaises with crisp white cushions are the picture of relaxation on the brick terrace.
OPPOSITE ❧ Ripening figs surround a glass-tile hurricane in an impromptu still life.

BEACH MOVIES

In these films, the location is as much a star as the actors. One of these could be just the mental vacation you need from winter—or inspiration for your next trip.

50 First Dates, Hanauma Bay, Oahu, Hawaii

Captain Corelli's Mandolin, Kefalonia, Greece

The Blue Lagoon, Port Antonio, Jamaica; Nanuya Levu Island, Fiji; Olu Deniz, Turkey; Turtle Island, Fiji

Mediterraneo, Kastelorizo Island, Dodecanese, Greece

Blue Crush, Oahu, Hawaii

Six Days, Seven Nights, Kauai, Hawaii

Summer Lovers, Greek Islands (Crete, Delos, Mykonos, Santorini)

Life as a House, Malibu, California

Something's Gotta Give, The Hamptons, New York

Pauline at the Beach, Granville, France

Message in a Bottle, Bath, Maine

How Stella Got Her Groove Back, Montego Bay, Jamaica

Cocktail, Ocho Rios, Jamaica

Y Tu Mama Tambien, Huatulco and Oaxaca, Mexico

Lifeguard, Torrance Beach, California

Wide Sargasso Sea, Jamaica

Summer of '42, Nantucket, Massachusetts

A Summer Place, Carmel-by-the-Sea, California

Swept Away, the Mediterranean (2002 version: Sardinia, Italy)

From Here to Eternity, Oahu, Hawaii

island living

DEE AND RANDY KRUSE ❧ LIDO ISLE, CALIFORNIA

Lido Isle is a tiny island—so small it was once just a sandbar—right off the coast of Newport Beach in California. Home to about eight hundred dwellings, it is entirely residential, with no stores, hotels, or even a gas station. This enclave was developed in the early 1930s as a European-style resort community modeled on Lido di Venezia, an island across the lagoon from Venice, Italy, but the Depression dampened sales, and only about fifty homes were built before World War II. By 1948, when Dee and Randy Kruse's home was built, about half the island had been developed. Now filled to the brim with homes that line *stradas,* or common walkways connecting the predominantly Mediterranean-style homes, Lido Isle is an idyllic and highly desirable,

albeit expensive, haven accessible by a bridge to the mainland. "There are lots of little inlets, parks, and docks, and a beach club," says Dee Kruse, describing the island's appeal. "In addition to the walkways that connect the homes, there is a main promenade that runs the length of the island, covered by a canopy of trees—it's very picturesque. The public school is great—it's one of only two in the United States on a beach. The best thing is when you drive home every day and see sailboats; it just feels so peaceful."

Dee and her husband, Randy, own a furnishings

PREVIOUS PAGE ⤚ The houses on Lido Isle are connected by pedestrian walkways, or *stradas*, that reduce vehicle traffic and forge close connections among neighbors. **LEFT** ⤚ Dee and Randy lightened the 1940s house by painting the ceiling beams white, widening doorways, and adding clean-lined French doors that open up the living and family rooms to the outdoors. **ABOVE** ⤚ Dee with her daughter, Bailey, and son, Jackson, at their favorite spot—the beach.

showroom and store in Newport Beach and do residential design as well. Their home had had a second floor added in the 1970s, creating a three-bedroom, 2,200-square-foot residence. After buying it in 2002, Dee and Randy took the house down to the studs. They kept the original footprint but opened up the space and gave the Spanish architecture a cleaner, updated feeling by adding more modern windows and French doors. They opened the kitchen to the living room and sandblasted the brick fireplace, which had been caked with paint. Avid gardeners, the Kruses introduced the plantings and fountain in their serene little courtyard.

As in her shop, Dee loves to mix old and new, juxta-

posing midcentury American and European designers with antiques and modern pieces. "If we had our druthers, we would probably have an all-white palette, but with two kids, we wanted to interject a little fun, color, and creativity," says Dee. The living room is a perfect case in point: Carved white chairs are upholstered in a bright grassy green chenille outdoor fabric that can stand up to the sun. "It felt natural to bring the green outside into the house," says Dee. The vintage leather horsehair-stuffed sofa from the late 1800s or early 1900s "adds a little soul and history to the room"; the brass and glass coffee table is midcentury, from Maison Jansen in Paris. While one might assume otherwise, the all-white room is actually the family room: "White slipcovers are easy to wash," points out Dee; the modern-icon Barcelona chairs are leather, and the coffee table is an indestructible Carrera marble plinth. Throughout the house, Dee and Randy painted the ceiling beams and rafters

ABOVE ⌁ Terra-cotta pavers from Spain on the side terrace suit the Mediterranean style of the house, with its tile roof and stucco walls.

OPPOSITE ⌁ Dee created a sitting area and home for art on the second-floor landing, carving a focal point and resting spot out of otherwise wasted space.

white instead of the traditional Mediterranean brown to keep rooms light, open, and airy.

Upstairs, even in the children's rooms, the mid-century aesthetic continues. A stripped-steel lawyer's cabinet from the 1950s is now home to a herd of dinosaurs in son Jackson's room, and pop-art prints line daughter Bailey's room. The master bathroom embodies the same cultural juxtapositions as the living room, with a deep rectangular sink (with both modern and vintage antecedents) atop an old wood table and beneath an ornate antique mirror in the crisp, limestone-walled room. The Kruses also chose limestone for the vintage-style basket-weave floor. "It's old and new, soulful and fresh," says Dee—the perfect leitmotif for their home.

When Dee decorates for the beach, both at home and for clients, she goes for "relaxed and livable," adding, "You don't want to be worried about things; it's not all so precious. You also have to keep in mind what

In the family room, white-slipcovered sofas and white leather Barcelona chairs are more child-friendly than they might seem at first glance. The Kruses swapped out the old windows and doors for simpler, more modern frames of stained knotty alder, and added dark wood shelves and cabinetry for books and the TV.

the salt water, sand, and wind do to everything."

For the Kruse family, the beach is an everyday way of life. "We ride our bikes to the beach almost every weekend," says Dee. "I grew up in Idaho and couldn't wait to get away from the cold winters. I moved to California when I was nineteen to go to school, and I never looked back."

ABOVE ⤳ Graphic pillows add punch to daughter Bailey's room.
RIGHT ⤳ Jackson's room eschews typical little-boy's-room patterns in favor of sophisticated cool with a sleek metal bed and lamp and framed skiing and motorcycle prints.

OPPOSITE ✦ In the master bath, a clean-lined Waterworks sink placed atop an old table contrasts with an ornate mirror. Limestone floor tiles update a classic basket-weave pattern.

ABOVE ✦ Dee and Randy added the cooling gurgle of a fountain and lush plantings to their courtyard. "It's our little getaway," Dee says.

RIGHT ✦ Antique candle sconces flank an encaustic painting by Maria O'Malley that picks up on the ebonized wood tones of the headboard in the master bedroom.

PAMPERING BEACH SPAS

Four Seasons Maui at Wailea, Hawaii

Las Ventanas al Paraiso, Los Cabos, Mexico

Kahala Mandarin Oriental, Oahu, Hawaii

Taha'a Pearl Beach Resort, Tahiti

Pangkor Laut, Malaysia

Taj Exotica Resort and Spa, Maldives

Four Seasons Resort, Santa Barbara, California

Hotel Hana-Maui, Hawaii

Malliouhana, Anguilla

The Cloister, Sea Island, Georgia

Four Seasons Nevis, West Indies

Maya Spa at Azulik, Tulum, Mexico

Carlisle Bay, Antigua

the collectors

shell game

HANNA STRUEVER ⤚ LAGUNA BEACH, CALIFORNIA

Hanna Struever remembers visiting her grandmother's house in Vero Beach, Florida, as a young girl, and being captivated by the bathroom vanity, a custom-built glass-topped counter filled with sand and beautiful shells. Fast-forward decades later: Hanna, a Michigan native, now lives in California and is a successful developer of luxury shopping centers around the world. Her office is in Laguna Beach, and she bought the small duplex cottage next door as a weekend retreat and guesthouse. "It's right on Victoria Beach, considered one of the gems of southern California," she explains. "It's kind of hidden and tucked away, with no parking, so it has stayed unspoiled. The beach, with its amazing tide pools and rock formations, overlooks Catalina Island, and

you can watch dolphins frolic and play in the water." The cottage was built in 1921, and unlike many of the neighboring houses that fill every inch of their compact lots, it boasts a wonderful hidden garden.

Hanna kept the house divided into two apartments to accommodate visiting family, friends, and colleagues, and decorated the light and airy upstairs floor in a crisp,

PREVIOUS PAGE ❧ The upstairs apartment has a crisp navy-and-white scheme. Hanna painted the beams with high-gloss white marine paint to lighten the formerly dreary space.
LEFT ❧ In the downstairs living room, Liz Garrett designed the shell-art fireplace mantel and shell frieze on the walls, which make this home a one-of-a-kind work of art.
ABOVE ❧ French doors, with breezy sheer curtains casually knotted, open the second-floor living room to the porch, where a small table for two offers outdoor dining.

nautically inspired navy-and-white palette. A charming porch off the living room affords water views. Downstairs, which is only about 800 square feet and has lower ceilings, Hanna took a cue from her grandmother's vanity and created a shell-lined jewel box of a home that is both cozier and a little more formal than the upstairs apartment.

Hanna works in a visual field, so she had a pretty clear idea of what she wanted and recruited a talented decorator, Liz Garrett, to help her fulfill her vision. Liz had created some shell art pieces that Hanna admired, and she enlisted Liz to cover the entire fireplace wall and mantel in a one-of-a-kind work of shell art (see "The Art of Shell Work," page 124). The starting point was a framed engraving of ships that hung on the wall, and over the course of numerous days, Liz arranged,

grouted, and glued hundreds of shells to the wall, framing the print in nautilus and scallop shells, which fit the luminescent white palette Hanna envisioned. Liz created the pattern as she went along, incorporating shell-and-coral candle sconces as well. She also lined the room in a starfish-and-scallop frieze and trimmed room-dividing curtains with a fringe of small shells. "Shells can be trinket-y and kitschy," says Hanna, "but Liz's skill is that she makes shell art sophisticated."

In the bedroom, Hanna showcased the talents of another artist, painter Tracey Moloney. "The ceilings are lower in the ground-floor unit than upstairs, and there was no easy way to change that, so I decided to embrace it as a design element, so that it feels cozy rather than cramped," explains Hanna. Tracey painted a trompe l'oeil striped tent on the ceiling, which makes the room feel taller, and painted scenes on the doors from the harbors of Capri and Saint-Tropez, some of

ABOVE A Javanese teak daybed on the upstairs porch provides a comfortable perch for ocean-gazing. Paisley and striped cushions create a summery study in blue and white. OPPOSITE Hanna camouflaged the low ceilings in the downstairs bedroom with a trompe l'oeil striped tent ceiling. Artist Tracey Moloney painted the harbor of Capri on the door.

THE OCEAN YACHT-RACE BETWEEN THE "CAMBRIA" AND THE "DAUNTLESS."

Hanna's favorite places from her travels. Saint-Tropez panoramas continue into the bathroom, where birds fly across a faux sky painted on the ceiling.

Upstairs, the blue-and-white stripes continue on upholstery and rugs, and there are subtler hints of the seaside in antique shell cases, crisp white walls, and high-gloss marine paint brightening the formerly dreary beamed ceiling. "I wanted to keep it clean and simple, without it being so simple that it looked temporary," says Hanna. "In small spaces, you have to choose one theme and repeat it—you don't have room to do lots of different things."

In Hanna's Laguna Beach home, the shells affixed to the first-floor walls not only root her home in its picturesque seaside setting but also "give it an individual feel and a sense of permanence. Sometimes beach houses look so predictable, as though everyone bought their furnishings from the same catalog or store," says Hanna. "I feel like this one is completely unique."

LEFT ✺ Using the framed sailboat engraving as a starting point, artist Liz Garrett created an elaborate shell-work mosaic including clamshell-and-coral candle sconces and rows of scallop shells outlining the mantel shelf.
OVERLEAF ✺ Liz made Hanna the charming "Casa del Mar"—"House of the Sea"—house sign as a gift.

the art of shell work

Sailors once created shell-encrusted "valentines"—boxes and plaques with detailed shell patterns—as a pastime to while away uneventful hours at sea and as mementos for their sweethearts back home. The Victorians were also known for crafting shell-covered curiosities and nautically inspired découpage. To bring the sometimes kitschy art of shell work into the modern day, decorator and artist Liz Garrett relies on symmetry, simplicity, and repetition, restricting her palette to certain colors and types of shells on each project. It all started with a mirror she created for her shop, Annie Magnolia, in Eureka, California, and then grew into boxes, valances, and this large-scale decorating project for Hanna. Surprisingly, Liz doesn't draw out a design ahead of time but rather mulls over the project in her head for a week or two, selects her shells, and then, when she's ready, starts the work and follows where it takes her.

For the fireplace, Liz had a mantel shelf attached to the wall and then covered everything in wire screening so she could use tile grout to securely affix the shells. "If the surface is too slick, the grout will crack and break off," she explains; the wire screening gives it traction. Working in daily shifts of about four hours at a time, it took her around thirty hours to complete the mantel. Liz used tiny shells, each one placed individually, to form the background of the design, then used larger scallop and nautilus shells to outline the framed artwork and the mantel and added jumbo scallop shells and coral to create the candle sconces. For smaller projects, like the starfish frieze, she hot-glued the shells directly to the wall.

Once she's finished her creations, Liz applies a clear polyurethane finish to protect them and give the shells an "ocean-washed" look: "Shells always look prettiest when they're wet and you can really see their colors."

SHE SELLS SEASHELLS . . .

Here are ome good online sources for buying shells:

Seashell City
708 Ocean Highway
Fenwick Island, DE 19944
(888) 743-5524
www.seashellcity.com

Sanibel Seashell Industries
1544 Periwinkle Way and
905 Fitzhugh Street
Sanibel, FL 33957
(239) 472-1603
www.seashells.com

U.S. Shell
Highway 100 and
Madison Street
Port Isabel, TX 78578
(800) 367-8508
www.usshell.com

Outer Banks Souvenirs
P.O. Box 1371
Nags Head, NC 27959
(252) 207-7737
www.outerbankssouvenirs.com

Starfish and Seashells
P.O. Box 612
Orange, CA 92856
(714) 849-0836
www.starfishandseashells.com

a perfect pair

BARCLAY BUTERA ✺ NEWPORT BEACH, CALIFORNIA

When it comes to beach houses, blue and white are the Ginger Rogers and Fred Astaire of decorating: natural partners, easy to work with, always right. Interior designer Barclay Butera takes decorating with blue and white to a new level, however, in his Newport Beach, California, home. While what he calls "sophisticated casual beach living" may not be casual to many people, the color scheme brings a simplicity of focus to his decorating. His home is a compact three-bedroom ranch built in the 1950s. Barclay ripped out the low ceilings, opening the space up to the rafters, and furnished the house in his signature style of layered patterns and textures.

Although each room is certainly put together with great care—the living/dining room alone boasts at least eight different fabrics—"If you think about it too much, it doesn't work," maintains Barclay. "I just choose textiles I like. I like to blend lots of materials and patterns and take risks. If you make a mistake, it's just a pillow. The overall look would not be effective if it weren't for all the layering."

Barclay isn't afraid to add pattern and texture on the walls, either. "I'm a big fan of wallpaper—I used it in every room," he says. "It's a simple way to bring dimen-

PREVIOUS PAGE ✎ Barclay had the ornate shell mirror custom-made for the grass cloth–lined entry. Framed fan coral and shells on the antique chest set a nautical tone.
LEFT ✎ The living room weaves together blue-and-white patterns, natural textures, and antiques with a confident hand. Clear glass lamp bases filled with sand and coral offer a modern counterpoint to framed shell engravings.
ABOVE ✎ An unusual shell chandelier helps define the dining area. Dark floors and furnishings create a dramatic backdrop for the play of blue and white.

sion and depth, or a whole different character, to a room." Ralph Lauren's classic blue-and-white Atelier Toile sets the stage in the living room, while a slightly softer blue paisley animates the master bedroom. Barclay cut the blue and white with lots of natural texture, such as sea-grass rugs, raffia-covered club chairs, a bamboo fire screen, and grass-cloth wallpaper (used even on the family-room ceiling). Board-and-batten paneling, rather than the expected bead board, gives the family room texture and warmth, while wood floors stained deep espresso inject contrast throughout the house. In the master bedroom, dark, carved mahogany furnishings lend a British Colonial flavor, leavened by the sky-blue wallcovering and bed linens.

Barclay is an inveterate collector, and his finds are showcased here in a nod to the seaside setting—shell

engravings flanking the fireplace, an intricate shell-covered mirror in the entry, and a shell chandelier over the dining table. He effortlessly mixes old and new, combining modern glass cylinder lamps and sleek cobalt hurricanes with antique blue-and-white export porcelain and maritime paintings. Orchids nestle in giant clams, and shells adorn everything from bottles to coasters, yet the effect is unquestionably sophisticated. "I enjoy showing people that you can design a beach house without getting kitschy," says Barclay. "This straddles the line between casual and grand."

French doors in the family room and dining room open up to a generous patio that is ideal for entertaining, with an outdoor fireplace and a luxurious spa in place of a pool. "I love this house because there are great places to gather and also rooms in which to retreat. The master suite is separate from the guest rooms, so everyone has privacy," says Barclay. "With everything

ABOVE ✐ Barclay raised the low ceilings to the rafters and painted them creamy white to "create a sense of openness." The family-room ceiling is papered in raffia. Board-and-batten paneling adds architectural detail. OPPOSITE ✐ Blue-and-white export porcelain, shell-covered bottles, coral, and maritime art create a seaside tableau.

on one level, it is easy to live in and maintain." Barclay moves frequently; this is his fifth house in the area. While each one allows him to further hone his take on beach-house style, he seems to have achieved perfection in this blue-and-white jewel box by the sea.

LEFT ☙ A beautiful blue paisley wallpaper in the master bedroom creates a serene retreat. The ceiling fan and carved four-poster bed impart a British Colonial flavor.
ABOVE ☙ Barclay created classic all-white baths using subway tile floor-to-ceiling with a hexagonal-tile floor. A built-in cabinet keeps towels and toiletries at the ready for guests.

a sense of history

SUZY AND RICHARD GROTE ～ NANTUCKET, MASSACHUSETTS

Nantucket is a world unto itself. Thirty miles off the coast of Massachusetts, only 14 miles long and 3½ miles wide, it was once the whaling capital of the world, a prosperous port and busy harbor from the mid-1700s to the late 1830s. Then petroleum was discovered, and whale oil was no longer needed for lamplight. Nantucket fell into a depression, and much of its population moved away.

That sudden reversal of fortune helped preserve the many eighteenth-century shingled and clapboard cottages, fine brick houses, and cobblestone streets through inattention. More recently, zealous preservation efforts and stringent regulations have protected the authenticity of the town. Nantucket's main business is now tourism,

and visitors continue to revel in its many beautiful beaches, its thousands of acres of nature preserves, and its picturesque villages of gray-shingled cottages wreathed in vivid purple-blue hydrangeas and pink climbing roses.

Suzy and Richard Grote's 1820s Federal-style house is one of those well-preserved historic houses. Suzy has a master's degree in architectural preserva-

PREVIOUS PAGE ❧ An antique Hitchcock bench welcomes guests in the front hall. The old-fashioned portrait of Liza and Peter as children was done by artist David Lancaster. The Twigs wallpaper, based on a period document, is a pattern that hung in Peter's room when he was a baby.
LEFT ❧ Horizontal plank walls in the renovated sitting room are less expected than bead board and provide texture and warmth for Suzy's collection of folk art.
ABOVE ❧ Adorned with mussel-shell and rope patterns and painted ships, this cupboard in the sitting room was made by a Nova Scotia artist. A sailor's valentine hangs above it.

tion from Columbia University, worked as a museum curator, and is now an interior designer, so the historical integrity of Nantucket Town holds special appeal for her. "The island is authentically old, which lends it a whole different feeling," says Suzy. She and Richard first visited Nantucket when they were living in New York in the 1970s. After a stint in London, they moved to Saint Louis, but they rented a summer house on Nantucket for a number of years. As their two children, Peter and Liza, got a little older, they decided to buy a house in the historic harbor town. They lived in their first house for twenty-two years; four years ago, they purchased this one.

Although it's not exactly a quick commute from Saint Louis to Nantucket, Suzy and Richard are enamored of the island's charms. They love picnic dinners on the beach (an island tradition), boating around the island, and peeking through the gates of other residences to marvel at the beauty of the gardens. Suzy does her best to make Nantucket her home base and run her business remotely in the summer, and the children, now in their late twenties, visit from New York and Boston.

When the Grotes bought this house, they wanted to preserve the original architecture as much as possible while removing an unattractive addition that had been put on in 1910. They kept the original house intact but reconfigured and rebuilt the back, within the same footprint, to include a renovated kitchen and sitting room, new baths, and updated heating and plumbing.

As they were renovating, Suzy began hunting down antiques from the same period as the house—Federal pieces from about 1810 to 1820, many in tiger maple, and she selected Twigs and Zoffany wallpapers based on period documents. She sought out art and

ABOVE ✦ In the dining room, antique Hitchcock chairs Suzy has collected gather around a reproduction table she had custom made. The wallpaper is another document pattern.

OPPOSITE ✦ Maple countertops and a hammered copper farm sink lend period warmth to the kitchen. A collection of Currier & Ives prints of children hangs on the wall.

accessories suited to the house and its location, like the paintings of sailing ships and the sailor's valentine (an intricate form of shell craft) in the sitting room, and the extraordinary cupboard patterned in mussel shells, with rope detailing and handpainted ship medallions, made by an artist in Nova Scotia. Her collections include small English teapots and pitchers from the 1820s to 1840s (which Americans would have collected in the era), antique hooked rugs, and Hitchcock chairs, which surround the dining table.

While antiques and fine fabrics might strike some as unbeachlike, they are perfectly suited to the historic character of Nantucket. "I wanted to decorate in a way that was appropriate to the house, but also cheery and bright," says Suzy. "I wanted it to feel airy and relaxed, not formal." Helping make the house beach-friendly are an outdoor shower for rinsing off sand, a back entrance and stairs, and a sunny yellow, casual third-floor bunk

room with plenty of sleeping space for kids and guests.

Suzy has managed to orchestrate a harmonious symphony of patterns in wallpaper, fabrics, and rugs that, while lively, is never overbearing. The walls are light, the designs are airy, and the color schemes are focused—with a gorgeous large-scale blue-and-white chinoiserie toile in the front parlor and soft sage green complemented by dusty red in the master bedroom. While there are pedigreed antiques in the house, nothing feels so precious that you can't sit on it or rest a drink on it. And modern amenities are welcomed: In the front parlor, Suzy cleverly tucked a bar with a mini-fridge into what was formerly a doorway to the den. The

OPPOSITE ❧ The wallpaper in the master bedroom is based on an 1820 Regency pattern. The unusual sampler on the wall is from the late 1880s; the quilt is also from the nineteenth century.
ABOVE ❧ An antique garden bench limns a lacy silhouette on the glossy white-painted floors of the renovated master bathroom.

all-white master bath possesses a contemporary simplicity, with glossy painted floorboards and the unexpected touch of an iron garden bench.

"We love Nantucket because it's a real town with a real community," says Suzy. "You can walk everywhere. You just head out the front door and amble down the cobblestone streets to find fantastic restaurants, shops, and diversions, which makes it easy to have guests. We're always meeting new and interesting people from all over. It's the best of beach *and* town."

ABOVE ✥ The 1820s Federal house has a clapboard front with a Greek revival doorway and shingled sides.
RIGHT ✥ The Grotes created a back porch from the former laundry room, where they often enjoy breakfast or entertain outdoors.

flotsam and jetsam

BOB AND PAM MELET ❧ MONTAUK, NEW YORK

Bob and Pam Melet named their daughter almost automatically—"We didn't even need to have a discussion," says Pam. Her name, Sunny, speaks volumes of their love for the beach. Ironically, Sunny was born with dark hair, but it soon grew in as a blond corona befitting her name, and now, at four years old, she is every bit as much of a beach lover as her parents. Bob and Pam met in Montauk, on the furthermost tip of Long Island, where Pam was renting this house and Bob was working while he styled the East Hampton store for Polo Ralph Lauren. Five years later, shortly after they were married, they learned that the owner of this two-story mother-daughter house (each floor is a separate apartment) was interested in selling. Pam recalls, "We were at the

Brimfield flea market, and we negotiated the price on a pay phone"—the perfect embodiment of their low-tech lifestyle. "That pay phone is still so special to us!"

The second floor is generally the most prized one in beach houses, because of the views. The previous owners, who had lived on that floor, decorated with everything faux—the complete antithesis of Bob and Pam's devotion to what is old and authentic. There were plastic seagulls on the walls, fake wood paneling, pressed wood furniture, plastic plants, and smoked-glass coffee tables, in a style probably unchanged since the house

PREVIOUS PAGE ✎ Stones collected on the beach, including black lava rock and some with hand-painted faces, have pride of place on a side table.
ABOVE ✎ Sunny, center, is a free spirit who loves the beach as much as Pam and Bob do.
RIGHT ✎ Bookshelves in the living room hold much more than books. They're layered with collections, like Bob's miniature outboard motors for model boats as well as antlers and other natural finds.

was built in the 1970s. Pam and Bob gave away a lot of things and gradually incorporated their own furnishings. They have yet to connect the two floors, but for now the setup works well for visiting friends and family.

Filled with the ever-changing finds of a professional collector, stylist, and some might even say hoarder, the house is a natural backdrop for Bob's distinctive and idiosyncratic collections of summer, such as miniature outboard motors made for model boats; skateboards from the 1960s and early '70s; and vintage Converse

LEFT ✎ Sunny, four years old, is following in the artistic footsteps of her parents, who have a passion for things that are handmade.
ABOVE ✎ Bob creates scrapbooks for Sunny from their trips to Mexico each year filled with photos and collages of detritus both natural and man-made.

high-tops. Pam and Sunny have added natural ephemera collected from the beach and surrounding woods, such as wave-smoothed stones, birds' nests, and antlers. When you see the sign Pam made when she first moved to the house and christened it Lovage, you know these two people were destined to meet. She crafted the letters from flotsam and jetsam such as driftwood, old rope, a heart-shaped rock, a crab claw, and a rubber ring.

Pam and Bob value emotional connections rather than perfection. "If either of us sees something that really moves us, we buy it, whether we have a place for it or not," says Pam. "We don't shop at malls. So much about the pieces we own is where they came from, where we were at that time in our life. That's what gives things meaning."

The house is two blocks from the ocean, and they can hear the symphony of its waves, especially during storms and in winter. In summer they scooter, bike, or

skateboard to the beach and spend the whole day there. "It's all about the beach here," says Pam, who is an avid surfer. "Our lives are so busy and complicated in the city. Out here I just like to sit. The beach is about family time. It's for fine-tuning the art of doing nothing. It's healthy to have that balance."

Even in winter, they love to bundle up and take walks on the narrow paths that traverse the cliffs by the beach. "It's black at night, there are no lights, and it's a completely different feeling," says Pam. Winter nights center around the fireplace. Come summer, the Melets

OPPOSITE ✿ Bob's collection of skateboards from the 1960s and early '70s is displayed vertically to show off their graphic tops as well as their wheels.
ABOVE ✿ The coffee table in the eclectically furnished living room is an old pig slaughter table. A wood box holds firewood; the garment rack serves as a coat closet.

are equally devoted to their outdoor shower. "We have one rule: You are not allowed to take an indoor shower in summer," says Pam. "It took a while for Bob's parents to get used to the idea, but now they are total converts. There is nothing better than taking a shower outside."

In the summer, they often drive out from their apartment in New York City late at night to avoid the Hamptons traffic, says Pam. "Then, once we're out here, everything just falls into place."

ABOVE ✲ Pam named her house "Lovage" and created this sign from old bits of flotsam and jetsam.
RIGHT ✲ A lodgepole bed Pam bought at a thrift shop takes up most of the tiny master bedroom. Pam painted the walls of the room red, then hung a Navajo rug on one wall, framing a silkscreen of a Native American chief.

SEASIDE SPORTS

For many of us, being at the beach is all about relaxing, reading, and napping. But the beach is also a great place to enjoy exercising in a glorious setting. When you're ready for a little action, there are plenty of fun sports meant to be enjoyed on the beach or in the water:

Volleyball
Paddleball/kadima
Boogie boarding
Beach biking (on special three-wheel reclining bikes)
Frisbee
Football
Swimming
Bodysurfing
Surfing
Sea kayaking
Sailing
Parasailing
Waterskiing
Snorkeling
Scuba diving
Windsurfing
Horseback riding
And, of course, walking and running

shipshape

Jeanne and Frank have lived abroad for much of their adult lives. Frank's work in the film business took them to Central America for many years, then to Italy and London. Forty some years ago, "we were living in the tropics in Panama, yearning for a northeastern storm and winters," says Jeanne. She traveled up to Cape Cod, looking for a small beach-house getaway to give them a foothold in the Northeast. She and Frank had both grown up in Boston and used to take day trips together to Cape Cod, out to Nauset Beach in Eastham. "Most people didn't go out that far," says Jeanne, referring to the long, curved hook at the far end of the Cape. "They might go to Falmouth or Osterville, but no one went past Orleans."

Jeanne remembered the natural beauty of the area from her earlier jaunts. "I spent several months looking on the Outer Cape. When we saw this house it was just a cinder-block bungalow, but it was in a stunning spot. The house is in a cove off Wellfleet Harbor, with hundred-eighty-degree views of the shoreline. And there is so much to look at—oyster beds and fishermen, tidal pools, islands out in the distance." So even though they could visit home only every three years and their summer vacations were wintertime in the

PREVIOUS PAGE ❧ A tower of hats in Jeanne and Frank's bedroom offers a variety of rakish options for sun protection.

LEFT ❧ One of several ship models they've collected lends a nautical air to the dining room. An old tripod light from a movie set stands in the corner. Jeanne and Frank added the wood ceilings and new windows to the house. With its compact spaces, wood trim, and views of water all around, "You feel like you're in a boat," says Jeanne.

ABOVE ❧ The house, which was added onto in sections, is perched atop the dunes overlooking Wellfleet Harbor.

Northeast, Jeanne and Frank purchased what turned out to be a wonderful home port for their family.

When they bought the house, their children were young—the last of the five hadn't even been born yet. Now the children are in their forties, with children of their own. Although they live as far afield as their parents once did—Florida, Los Angeles, New York, London, and France—they still come to visit in Wellfleet, where Jeanne and Frank live five months of the year.

Over the decades, they made upgrades to the house. "We've had about six episodes of renovation," Jeanne says. They planted evergreen shrubs on the dunes leading down to the water to buffer the house from strong, gusty winds and help protect it during storms. "When we would arrive, we'd have to shovel the sand away from the windows. The glass was pitted from all the sand blowing up against it," remembers Jeanne. "After ten or fifteen years, we put in heat—before that there was only a fireplace—and thermal pane windows."

As the family has evolved, so has the house. What was once the children's playroom has been converted into an indoor-outdoor lap pool with a double-glazed garage door that opens the pool up to the outdoors. The master bedroom and bath and a small shaded porch are now secluded at the far end of the house, which creates a nice buffer of privacy when everyone comes to visit. And what was once a sleeping loft for the kids became a sitting room with breathtaking views.

"We've always had an open kitchen in the center of the house," says Jeanne. "That way, whoever's cooking is not abandoned while everyone else goes off to have drinks—they're surrounded by people sitting on the banquette and at the counter, chopping, chatting, and helping." When the architecture firm Pierce/Allen worked

ABOVE ☞ Framed ship paintings and prints of whales and shells underscore the nautical theme. The cabana-stripe banquette invites guests to gather in the kitchen.
OPPOSITE ☞ A bump-out was added to accommodate a circular table surrounded by a built-in banquette. much like the compact dining quarters on a boat.

on the most recent renovation of the house, they added a bump-out to the kitchen/dining area, with a curved bay of windows and a round table encircled by a built-in banquette. "The grandchildren love to eat there," says Jeanne.

Other nods to the family's love of sailing include wood ship models, antique nautical maps of the area, old ship's lanterns, and watercolors and prints of ships and fish, some taken from the many books they've collected. "On Sunday mornings we like to go to the Wellfleet flea market. Over the years, whenever we saw an old map of Cape Cod we liked, or an interesting book, we picked it up," says Jeanne. A wood case filled with old fishing lures on the sitting room table was a gift from their son and daughter-in-law. Though the family once raced Lightning sailboats in the harbor, now Jeanne and Frank have a motorboat for easy jaunts.

A nautically inspired palette of blue and white wafts through the house: crisp cabana stripes on the

LEFT ⚓ Jeanne and Frank transformed the former playroom into an indoor/outdoor lap pool overlooking the water. A double-glazed glass-paned garage door slides down to create an indoor heated pool in winter. A small deck offers seating and a glorious view in nice weather.

all around it, yet it is snug and inviting when it's chilly or stormy. With no superhighway access, Wellfleet is remote enough that it's not overcrowded, but it's picturesquely reachable from Boston via a catamaran ferry to Provincetown. Even today, more than forty years after Jeanne and Frank bought the house, the area is little changed. Strict town planning laws and environmental restrictions have protected this natural gem. "In a way, it's unfair, because not many people can buy here," says Jeanne, referring to the lack of development and the resulting high prices of the houses that exist. But that careful stewardship has also ensured that Wellfleet has retained its natural splendor and simplicity. "It's an incredibly beautiful, natural spot," says Jeanne. "You can go biking, kayaking, hiking, or sailing. And the air is wonderful—a crisp combination of salt air and pine trees that I find very therapeutic"—a therapy of the most appealing kind.

kitchen banquette; a handsome, cozy blue plaid on the sitting room furniture; and vintage chenille bedspreads in the guest room. The warmth of natural wood everywhere, like the brightwork on a boat, is balanced by white walls, the lack of clutter, and the irresistible views that constantly draw the eye outward. Nothing is particularly precious, but the house has the clean, trim lines of a well-designed yacht.

It is hard to imagine a more ideal spot. The house is secluded from its neighbors by dint of its dune-top setting; it is like the prow of boat, overlooking the water

ABOVE ✺ The house is connected by outdoor decks. This seating area is between the dining room and master bedroom. The staircase leads to Frank's office.
OPPOSITE ✺ An enticing view: A long set of stairs with rope handrails leads from the house down to the beach and the sparkling bay.

DANGER
DEEP
WATER

the purists

art of improvisation

FIONA DUFF KAHN AND ROBERT KAHN ✒ WAINSCOTT, NEW YORK

This small shingled cottage—just a shack, really—that belongs to Fiona Duff Kahn and her husband, Robert Kahn, is a miraculous holdout from the developers' wrecking ball that has leveled so many of its compatriots among the increasingly valuable properties of New York's fabled Hamptons. It helps that it is in Wainscott, a tiny, low-key community sandwiched between East Hampton and Bridgehampton that until recently wasn't really on the Hamptons radar. Nestled on a small piece of property shaded by giant pines and thick rhododendrons that borders on a farm, the house has expansive views that belie its small size. It's within biking distance of the beach, and when it's quiet, you can hear the ocean, but it feels more like a cabin in the woods.

The house was most likely a prototype of a 1940s Abercrombie & Fitch kit house that came in numbered pieces with slots. "There's not a nail in the house," says Fiona. Just 700 square feet with two bedrooms, it was built in 1947, and a spacious screened porch was added in 1952, which granted another 400 square feet of living, lounging, and dining space to the tiny bungalow.

Fiona's husband, Bob, is an architect, but this house is more her domain, left deliberately unimproved, to keep life as simple as possible. There is no electricity on the porch, which invites "beautiful dinners where the whole place is lit up by candles," and there's no heat, so

PREVIOUS PAGE Fiona still makes mobiles from shells she finds on the beach, just as she did when she was a child. ABOVE The little cottage, built in 1947, is one of the few that have not succumbed to the wrecking ball in the Hamptons. RIGHT A screened porch built in the 1950s adds another 400 square feet of outdoor living space to the house. Fiona found the rattan furniture at a little shop in New York.

it's purely a summerhouse, with a cast-iron stove for chilly nights in spring and fall.

"The house is underbuilt, whereas houses today tend to be overbuilt and all sealed up," says Fiona. "The walls were unfinished; you could see the studs, which are only one-by-twos. The asphalt roof had been repaired with heavy-duty aluminum foil! There was nothing but brown kraft paper lining the inside of the clapboard exterior. It felt almost porous." Fiona did make a few changes to the house: "Everything was brown, and you couldn't see a thing without turning on the lights," so she added bead-board paneling inside and painted it white, which brightened up the interior significantly, and then chose a friendly palette of 1940s colors for the floors, furnishings, and curtains. The living room floor is robin's-egg blue, the guest room floor mossy green, and the bedroom floor calamine pink; there are touches of forest green (on a vintage refrigerator and claw-foot

tub), and yellow and cheery red gingham on the ruffled curtains. Furnishings were either in the house already, or are tag-sale or flea-market finds, an amiable beach-house jumble. There are no modern conveniences like a dishwasher, washer and dryer, or TV, which suits them just fine. Life steps back half a century here to a simpler time when clothes dried on the line and kids entertained themselves collecting shells, building sandcastles, or playing cards.

OPPOSITE ← The kitchen is, true to period, a hodgepodge of individual elements: The sink is original, as are the odds-and-ends of cabinets, and the appliances are vintage. Fiona added open shelves along one wall to serve as a pantry. Red gingham curtains add a cheery note.
ABOVE ← The delicious fresh flavors of summer are culled from local farm stands and a good fish store nearby.

To Fiona and her family, including her four-year-old daughter, Kiki, the house feels larger than its diminutive size because "there are so many different places to hang out—the porch, the living room, a hammock and swing on one side of the house, and Adirondack chairs and picnic table on another," says Fiona. "The porch is a perfect napping spot—you just get into the hammock and pretend you are going to read in the perfect green,

LEFT ✦ Sign of an earlier time: Laundry drying on the line.
ABOVE ✦ The porch serves as the dining room, and with no electricity, is romantically lit by candlelight at night.

shady light." They never know what the farmer next door is going to plant. Some years it's corn; this year it was a remarkable field of big sunflowers that made them feel as if they were living in Provence.

The house has the feel of serendipity about it, probably because Fiona and Bob have put such a light footprint on it. "It feels like we inherited it in a way," says Fiona. "You get to know the people who lived here before you through a house, while in the process, you make it your own."

ABOVE RIGHT ✍ The house has the good fortune to border on a farm, which, this summer, was filled with a glorious crop of van Gogh–like sunflowers.
RIGHT ✍ Nothing is precious: All the furnishings were either already there or bought at yard sales or junk shops. The original cast-iron stove still works. Fiona put up the bead board and painted it white to brighten the cabin.

READ ALL ABOUT IT: LIFE AT THE BEACH

When you can't be at the beach, read about it. These books celebrate the fantasy of life by the water, even as they sometimes reveal the less picturesque realities.

The Big House: A Century in the Life of an American Summer Home, by George Howe Colt

The Salt House: A Summer on the Dunes of Cape Cod, by Cynthia Huntington

A Year by the Sea: Thoughts of an Unfinished Woman, by Joan Anderson

Gift from the Sea, by Anne Morrow Lindbergh

Beach: Stories by the Sand and Sea, edited by Lena Lencek and Gideon Bosker

Summer, by Alice Gordon and Vincent Virga

In a House by the Sea, by Sandy Gingras

An Embarrassment of Mangoes: A Caribbean Interlude, by Ann Vanderhoof

A Trip to the Beach: Living on Island Time in the Caribbean, by Melinda Blanchard and Robert Blanchard

The Outermost House: A Year of Life on the Great Beach of Cape Cod, by Henry Beston

Very California: Travels Through the Golden State, written and illustrated by Diana Hollingsworth Gessler

The Beach: The History of Paradise on Earth, by Lena Lencek and Gideon Bosker

Hamptons Bohemia: Two Centuries of Artists and Writers at the Beach, by Helen A. Harrison and Constance Ayers Denne

Beaches (photographs), edited by Gideon Bosker and Lena Lencek

Cape Light: Color Photographs, by Joel Meyerowitz

BEACH READS

By definition, beach reads should be page-turners—not too taxing on the brain but impossible to put down. Here are some good reads that are themselves set on the coast:

Skinny Dip, by Carl Hiassen

The Beach, by Alex Garland

The Beach House, by James Patterson and Peter de Jonge

Beachcombing for a Shipwrecked God, by Joe Coomer

The Perfect Storm, by Sebastian Junger

Philistines at the Hedgerow, by Steven Gaines

Message in a Bottle, by Nicholas Sparks

The Weight of Water, by Anita Shreve

Amagansett, by Mark Mills

The Beach Club, Summer People, and other books by Elin Hilderbrand

Savannah Breeze, by Mary Kay Andrews

Coast Road, by Barbara Delinsky

Sea Swept, Rising Tide, and *Inner Harbor,* by Nora Roberts

Hawaii, by James Michener

Jaws and *White Shark,* by Peter Benchley

all natural

MARSIA AND LEONARD HOLZER ❧ WATER MILL, NEW YORK

Looking at this beautiful shingle-style house on a multimillion-dollar beachfront property in the Hamptons, with its gorgeous pool and lush gardens, you might expect the inside to be furnished to the nines by an interior designer, with fine furniture, lavish window treatments, rugs, and accessories. In fact, it is furnished in the simple, pared-down, and relaxed style of a humble beach cottage, which contributes in large part to its refreshing charm.

The original house was built in 1910. More recent improvements include a renovated kitchen and French doors added by the previous architect-owner. Marsia and Leonard Holzer bought the house in 1991 and added the

glorious pool as well as the crisp white railings across the porch and deck, but otherwise kept the house much as it was. Marsia quickly set to work transforming the scrubby dunes into a terraced garden reminiscent of ones in her native England. "I wanted to have an herbaceous border like my mother's, but nothing survived the salt air and wind out here, so you learn what you can and can't grow," says Marsia. "I brought in truckloads of topsoil, created terraces with small stone walls, and planted a cutting

PREVIOUS PAGE ✷ On the front porch, Adirondack chairs and a rattan couch offer "a lovely place to sit and watch the ocean," says Marsia.
ABOVE ✷ Marsia and her dog, fellow beach lovers.
RIGHT ✷ Undressed windows, pickled maple moldings, white walls, and pale furnishings keep the living room light and informal. Marsia made the bronze tree lamp.

garden of flowers and an organic vegetable garden," which provides fresh tomatoes, English peas, beans, salad greens, and herbs for the table all summer long.

Marsia is an energetic outdoorswoman who relishes their waterfront location primarily for its proximity to the activities she loves—kayaking on Mecox Bay, bicycling, horseback riding, and walking on the beach. "There's so much to do out here, and the air and light are so fabulous," she enthuses. "I bike a lot—I have a hybrid bike and a sports bike—and I train for hundred-mile races. I'll bike over to friends and then we'll bike for half a day. My daughter and I both have horses and love to ride. I'm half Scottish and half English, so I love to hike and walk on the beach. And I love to cook and entertain." All this from a woman who has three grown children!

Leonard and Marsia's children, now in their twenties and early thirties, come out to visit often, as do friends and extended family, and that's just how they like it. "We're crammed with people all the time," says Marsia, and they accommodate them with five small bedrooms in the main house; a one-bedroom apartment with two futons and a sofa bed over the garage; built-in cedar banquettes that people can sleep on in the pool house; and camp beds in the basement to handle the overflow.

Marsia trained as a fine artist, had a career in fashion as a costume designer, and then recently sidestepped into furniture and lighting design. "I don't like to shop," she notes. "I'd rather make what I need." She started by crafting paper lanterns for her home. One day, she created an airplane out of parchment that flew

OPPOSITE ⬿ Once "a scrubby dune," the beautifully terraced garden is Marsia's handiwork, where she grows flowers that can tolerate the salt air, and herbs and organic vegetables that make their way to her table.
ABOVE ⬿ Marsia cast the aluminum lamp on a demilune table in the dining room from driftwood she found while kayaking.

across the cloudy gray "sky" of her foyer ceiling with a lightbulb in place of its engine. "I took a welding class so I could learn how to join the wings," recalls Marsia, and from there she began creating lamps as well as large metal sculptures of horses, her great love. She casts driftwood and fallen branches she finds kayaking into bronze and aluminum lamp bases. "My lighting has often been about things found in nature. Even the shades are mica," says Marsia. A trip to Costa Rica inspired yet another passion. She discovered a huge, beautiful tree that had fallen down in the rain forest,

ABOVE ⤚ When not outside, dinners take place around a long Shaker dining table surrounded by old wicker chairs Marsia spray-painted white to unify. Wood ducks swim on a sea of fava beans down the center of the table.

RIGHT ⤚ The kitchen is lined mostly with windows rather than upper cabinets. "It's fabulous to be able to look out at the water as I'm cooking," says Marsia.

arranged to have it shipped back to her studio in New York City, and began creating tables, headboards, and other furnishings that celebrate the organic beauty of the wood.

The Holzers' relaxed, unpretentious home reflects their appreciation for nature. They had the first-story floors and moldings stripped down to bare maple and then pickled, to give them the feeling of driftwood. Paintings of shore birds, some by Michael Vollbracht, a fellow fashion designer and artist, and carved wood ducks, some of which belonged to Marsia's aunt, are scattered throughout the house. Large shells collected at roadside shell stores in Florida take pride of place in the dining room cupboard. Marsia made the headboard in the master bedroom from wood she found on the beach and cut in slices. In the kitchen sits a big 20-inch jar filled with sea glass that she and her daughter began collecting when her daughter was eight. "We said, 'Let's see if we can fill this up by the time you go to college,'"

recalls Marsia, which they did (her daughter is now twenty-one). Marsia laments that it's harder and harder to find sea glass now that so many things are made of plastic.

In this house, little is precious in the traditional sense of the word. Perhaps the splashiest room is the bath, which was designed by the previous owner. Lined in luminous turquoise tiles, it gives the feeling of being submerged undersea.

But the Holzers' favorite place to be is usually the front porch overlooking the ocean: "It's such a lovely place to sit," says Marsia. "You're so close to the waves, it's like being on board a ship."

OPPOSITE ✎ Marsia gave Leonard this Eames chair for his birthday. He often has to be on the phone with patients, so it's positioned in a quiet spot in their bedroom where he can sit and enjoy the view while working.
ABOVE ✎ Marsia made the headboard in the master bedroom from a tree trunk found on the beach.

ABOVE ❧ The luminous turquoise tile in the master bath, installed by the previous owner, echoes the feeling of the pool, or as Marsia says, "It's like taking a shower in a big Navajo belt."

RIGHT ❧ The Holzers added the pool for windy days and for those not inclined to swim in the ocean. Surrounded by canvas umbrellas and teak chaises, it feels as inviting as a resort. Marsia, an avid outdoorswoman, swims one half to a full mile each day in it.

OPPOSITE ✦ Having lunch or dinner *en plein air*, beneath the shade of a striped umbrella, provides a breathtaking view of the ocean. The table is just outside the kitchen for easy serving.

ABOVE ✦ Old Glory in full glory, on the back porch of the house.

SMALL PLEASURES

This is what being at the beach is all about:

Smelling the salt air

Feeling the sun warm your skin

Jumping the waves

Finding a beautiful shell

Digging your toes into the sand

Getting a whiff of Coppertone

Drifting in and out of sleep as you lie on your towel

Floating in salt water

Bodysurfing the perfect wave

Taking a long walk at sunset

Watching a thunder and lightning storm move across the water from the safety of a porch

Showering outdoors

Looking out from the top of a Ferris wheel

Making a sandcastle

Watching the fireworks

Getting on the ferry

Waking up early and watching the sunrise

Enjoying the cool shade of an umbrella on a hot afternoon

Sipping an ice-filled drink on the beach

Screaming at the top of your lungs on the roller coaster

Playing Monopoly or Scrabble on a rainy day

Riding an old bike that doesn't have to be locked up

Eating the very freshest fish or crabs or lobster (especially if you caught it yourself)

Not having to leave on Sunday, but staying for the whole week . . . or month . . . or summer

attention to detail

LENNY AND BOB STEINBERG ✲ VENICE, CALIFORNIA

Lenny Steinberg, an architectural designer, and her husband, Bob, have been coming to Venice Beach, California, for more than twenty-five years. "We lived in Beverly Hills, but we always had a cottage or condo, a small something at the beach," says Lenny. "We finally decided it was time to live year-round in this amazing community of artists. We had an apartment in the West Village in Manhattan for many years, and Venice has a similar combination of old and new, interesting people and passing parades, and the ability to walk to restaurants and galleries. It's like the vicarious feel of a city at the beach."

The Steinbergs found a beachfront house that had been built in the mid 1970s; like many of the homes in

Venice, it was a duplex. "I knew the house, and we loved the location," says Lenny. It's on Ocean Front Walk, but on a noncommercial stretch six or eight blocks away from the crowds. "This area has come to be known as 'architect's row,'" says Lenny. One of the first houses Frank Gehry designed is three doors down, and nearby houses were designed by Antoine Predock and Steven Ehrlich.

PREVIOUS PAGE ✥ Sixteen-foot-high windows, with doors that recess into the walls on each side, literally open the house up to the beach.
LEFT ✥ Modular seating and a table on wheels of Lenny's own design offer highly flexible arrangements.
ABOVE ✥ Lenny renovated a beachfront duplex into a loft-like single-family home with an expansive glass front across its stucco exterior.

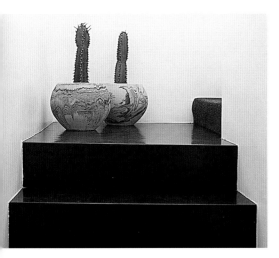

"Each of the houses here is on the same small twenty-eight-foot-wide lot. We were fortunate in that we have an eight-foot easement, which allows us a bit of a garden, and the front of the house faces a walk street with no traffic," says Lenny. She combined the duplex apartments into one house, opened it up, and added a 16-foot-high glass front. Breaking out of the rectangular grid, she designed the front of the house on a slight angle to expand the view south to the pier at Washington Boulevard. Vertical planes like the sides of the front deck and the bedroom/library loft are slightly canted "so the edges open up and breathe a bit."

The house's low-ceilinged entrance accentuates the drama as you progress into the soaring double-height living space with a front-row view of the beach and ocean. On nice days, the Steinbergs can slide the large glass doors into the walls to open up the room completely to the outdoors. The main room incorporates living, dining, and kitchen areas. A second-floor loft extending partway over the kitchen houses a library and the master bedroom, which creates a more intimate oasis within the larger space. A lower level houses a guest suite that's as refined as any boutique hotel, and Lenny added a staircase to the roof and created a spacious rooftop patio with spectacular views.

For all the grand gestures she incorporated into the house, Lenny also paid incredible attention to small details, such as a staircase that winds around "so there's not a long stretch of stairs that looks wearisome, as it can in a three-story house." The fireplace hearth is raised about 14 inches and extends to become the second step of the stairs. Lenny set the pattern of the North Carolina bluestone floors herself, fashioning the slabs to give the subtle effect of a river flowing toward

ABOVE ✺ Lenny designed the staircase that joins the three stories of the house so that it is slowly revealed as you turn corners, rather than "one wearisome, long line of stairs." This set of stairs leads to the rooftop terrace.
OPPOSITE ✺ Lenny reinforced the second-story ceilings so she could create a rooftop terrace, with an outdoor shower, a hot tub, a seating area, and spectacular views.

the ocean, subliminally drawing you toward the view. She even took care to hide all the light switches.

Lenny is also a distinguished furniture designer, and nearly all the pieces in the house are her own designs, including the modular sofas in the living room that can be arranged in any number of configurations. They are covered in an indestructible fabric used in Mercedes cars, a boon in a beach house. A similarly versatile pair of metallic-glazed angled dining tables can be used separately, joined end to end, or set in a square, and a long granite-and-iron table on wheels perfectly suits "a house that invites change," as Lenny describes it.

She delights in discovering new materials or using them in unexpected ways, as in the sculptural kitchen island she made from a sand-and-epoxy composition material intended for industrial flooring. Its pale platinum hue is "almost the color of ocean foam," says Lenny. She cleverly incorporated everything except the kitchen sink into the island, including wine drawers, a built-in toaster compartment, the cooktop, and storage cabi-

The glass doors in the living area recess into side pockets so that the house can be fully opened to the outdoors for beachfront dining or lounging with all the comforts of home.

thrive on it. "It's wonderful people-watching; it's always busy," says Lenny. "I love observing the ritual of the surfers heading down to the ocean in the morning, or the people practicing tai chi on the beach. It's an ever-changing panorama." A solid front on the Steinbergs' deck, rather than the glass fronts many other homes boast, permits them to see out without letting passersby see in, an option that affords a measure of privacy in a fairly public location.

Living on the ocean, Lenny says, "every day is a wonderment. I never get tired of seeing the sunset." The truest measure of the success of this house: "Wherever we've traveled in the world, we come home and say, 'Why go away? What could be better than this?'"

nets. Beautiful antique wood doors from Japan conceal a pantry and shelves for dishes and glassware along one wall. Those same Japanese doors reappear fronting closets in the bedroom. Lenny often repeats materials used in one place in subtle variations elsewhere in the house, like the large slab of quartzite that serves as an exterior step and is carried through inside as insets in the floor. A ribbon of windows on the side wall is Lenny's homage to Pierre Chareau's Maison de Verre; it is repeated in the library and bathrooms.

Though some might find Venice's weekend crowds and activity level too frenetic, the Steinbergs seem to

ABOVE ✐ A small dining terrace extends off the back of the house, emphasizing its indoor/outdoor nature.
OPPOSITE ✐ The kitchen island is fabricated from a composition material commonly used for industrial flooring. Drawers for wine storage and a toaster compartment are built into one end. Antique Japanese doors behind the island conceal storage. Lenny collects the beautiful marbleized pottery known as "roadside pottery," made by Mexicans and Native Americans in the late 1920s and sold to tourists by the side of the road.

beach-house elements

Whether you live by the water, or just want the relaxed, summery look and feel of beach house style inland, here are key ingredients that can give any home an instant dose of sunshine, pleasure, and

furnishings

CHAISE LOUNGE

The chaise lounge is the most coveted spot in the summer—the perfect perch for relaxation and the only truly comfortable way to recline while reading a book, sipping a drink, or staring out at the ocean. The most pampering chaises, whether teak, iron, or aluminum, have plump cushions (best when covered in all-weather fabric), though there are fine-mesh versions that are supportive and soft as well (a far cry from the woven nylon-strap chaise lounges of old). Similarly, the steamer chair—generally a folding wood chaise that was once used on the decks of ocean liners—offers lounging with sophistication.

Indoors, an upholstered chaise lounge offers the same kind of inviting indulgence to a corner of the bedroom or living room.

SLIPCOVERS

Slipcovers have been used to protect fine upholstery fabrics from the sun since at least the eighteenth century in England. They also have long been used to give heavy upholstery such as velvets and wools a softer touch in summer, with airy white cottons and linens that feel cooler on bare skin. Slipcovers in a beach house, whether of white canvas or a simple ticking stripe, give furnishings a more relaxed persona; they also offer the practical bonus of being washable and able to stand up to sandy feet and damp bathing suits. They are a relatively inexpensive way to unify or dress up disparate pieces of secondhand furniture, or to change the look of a room with the season. In short, their crisp simplicity and lack of affectation make them summerhouse naturals.

WICKER FURNITURE

Wicker is a naturally cooling material for summer and seaside furniture because it allows air to circulate, is lightweight, and resists moisture and humidity. Wicker furniture may be made from willow, cane, rattan, reed, or man-made fibers. Woven willow furniture dates back to ancient Roman times, but cane, rattan, and reed furnishings came into their heyday at the turn of the twentieth century. Wicker furniture became popular during the Victorian era for porches, conservatories, and gardens. Designs became quite ornate, with intricate and fanciful patterns woven into seat backs and tabletops. Wicker was also used for seats on cruise ships, trains, cars, and airplanes. After World War I, mass-produced wicker furnishings became readily available at lower prices, but the intricacy of the designs greatly diminished. Whether new or antique, wicker furniture lends a gracious air of gentility to patios, screened porches, and covered decks, as well as indoor rooms. It can be easily painted, and cushions add to its comfort and design flexibility.

SEA-GRASS AND SISAL RUGS

Natural fiber rugs woven of materials such as sisal, sea grass, hemp, coir, abaca, jute, and bamboo have become incredibly popular in recent years due to the simple, neutral background they confer and their versatility in working with a wide range of styles. Their sturdy weaves and sandy neutral color make them a favorite choice for beach homes. Keep in mind that all natural fibers, particularly sea grass and jute, absorb moisture easily, and should not be used in very damp or humid environments like bathrooms, kitchens, or basements, where they are subjected to mold and mildew.

Sisal and coir are among the sturdiest rugs, while jute is more delicate, and abaca is known for its resistance to salt water. Direct sunlight can fade or darken natural fibers over time, so rugs should be rotated periodically. In a room where furniture is moved regularly (such as a dining room), flat-weave rugs, which don't show indentations as easily as narrow bouclé weaves, are preferable.

PLANTER'S CHAIR

The planter's chair was a common feature in Caribbean plantations, but variations of it can be found in tropical colonial outposts all over the world. It is usually made of teak, with a sloping, curved cane seat and back (all of one piece), with long arms. The arms often fold out and extend, so that the planter, hot and tired after a day on horseback surveying his fields, could prop his swollen feet up on the chair arms, and have his boots pulled off more easily. Today, the planter's chair is still an elegant and cooling response to hot climates, with its

caned seating, which allows air to circulate, and reclining form.

ADIRONDACK CHAIR

No one knows for sure the provenance of the Adirondack chair, and whether it even originated in the Adirondacks, but it became particularly popular before and after World War I as the middle class began to enjoy summer camps, resorts, and outdoor living. Its sturdy slat wood construction made it easy and inexpensive for local craftsmen to produce. Today it is a favorite for decks, lawns, and docks, with its angled back (curved-back variations are even more comfortable) and wide arms, which offer a natural perch for drinks.

HAMMOCK

Lounging in the comforting embrace of a hammock on a sultry summer afternoon may well represent the apogee of leisure. Rope hammocks were originally devised as portable beds on ships, so it's appropriate that they offer a

home for nappers by the sea. There are all sorts of accoutrements for hammocks—small pillows, drink holders, magazine caddies, canopies—but the simplest ones of rope or canvas suffice quite well alone. Perhaps the most well known hammock is the Pawleys Island rope hammock, which originated in 1889 in Pawleys Island, South Carolina, when a river boat captain decided to create a cooler alternative to the grass-filled mattress on his boat.

CANVAS UMBRELLA

Like its brethren on the beach, a canvas umbrella used on a deck or with an outdoor table is an inviting and often essential source of shade and respite from the bright summer sun. Canvas beach umbrellas (as well as chairs and cabanas) in distinctive multicolored stripes were first a fixture on the Riviera; soon they were adopted in the United States as middle-class citizens began going to the beach in larger numbers beginning in the 1930s.

Today, umbrellas make any outdoor space, particularly dining areas, feel more welcoming and protected.

PICNIC TABLE AND BENCHES

A backyard classic, the picnic table is equally at home on beaches and decks, where its built-in benches and sturdy form make it weather-resistant and child-friendly. It is a relatively inexpensive, practical way to seat a crowd.

DECK CHAIR

Descendants of folding military campaign furniture, variations on the deck or director's chair have been around for centuries, and are still popular at home and on boats because they are lightweight; easy to fold, transport, and store; and relatively inexpensive. Their canvas seats make them comfortable and light in summer, and it is always easy to pull up a few more around a table for an alfresco meal.

architectural elements

DECK, PORCH, VERANDA, OR PATIO

Whatever you choose to call it, every beach house should have a place to sit, relax, eat, read, and

relish the outdoors. This halfway house between indoors and out is often the most cherished place to be. It may be screened or covered to offer a greater sense of shelter (especially appreciated in the rain or strong sun), or completely open (with perhaps an umbrella, an awning, or a pergola for shade) for the more full-on experience of being outdoors. Many amenities have been devised to enhance the patio and deck, from elaborate outdoor kitchens (with mini-fridge, stovetop, and more) to fire pits, hot tubs, built-in seating, and beautiful plantings. But even the simplest porch with a comfortable chair offers all that's really needed to soak up the pleasures of being outside, yet close to all the comforts of home.

CEILING FAN

These days, there are more and more beach houses with air-conditioning, but one of the benefits of living near the water, after all, is cooling ocean breezes. So for all but the hottest days, let Mother Nature provide the AC, with a nudge from the soft, sultry whir of a ceiling fan. Not only is it fresher, less expensive, and more romantic, you'll be helping save the planet to boot.

SCREEN DOOR

Swish, slap, swish, slap—the syncopation of a screen door opening and closing provides a nostalgic sound track for the life of a summer house. Instead of sealing the house off from outside life, a screen door welcomes salt-air breezes and the

sounds of birdsong inside, while keeping pests at bay. Wood doors are preferable to aluminum ones, for sonorous as well as aesthetic reasons.

PLANTATION SHUTTERS

Borrowed from tropical island architecture, plantation shutters have a clean elegance as well as practical utility. Their wide (usually 2- or 3-inch) slats filter the sun while still allowing air through. Less fussy than curtains, they project a graphic play of shadow and light across the floor. Plantation shutters are usually made in two single panels, rather than bifold panels, across the window. They can be crisp and white, or take on a more British Colonial richness in mahogany or other woods.

OUTDOOR SHOWER

This is perhaps the simplest of luxuries, yet to its aficionados, one of the greatest pleasures of summer at the beach. The experience of bathing *en plein air*, yet with the protective modesty of a wood surround, offers an elemental freedom that must harken back to bathing in streams and lakes before indoor plumbing was invented. Outdoor showers provide the convenience of washing off all the sand before you traipse into the house, and the bracing refreshment of a warm shower in cooler air (or vice versa). Plant some mint around your shower and enjoy a little aromatherapy as well.

OUTDOOR FIREPLACE

Like an outdoor shower, an outdoor fireplace offers the perfect combination of warmth with chill. When it's early or late in the

season, and the temperature dips at night, burning wood in a fire pit (usually a low, shallow bowl made of metal) or *chimnea* (a terra-cotta or cast-iron fireplace that originated in Mexico) offers guests glowing warmth and caters to a primal urge to gather around the fire. Both the fire pit and the *chimnea* are transportable, storable, and relatively inexpensive, while an outdoor fireplace made of stone and masonry is an inviting but more permanent architectural addition to your patio.

SWIMMING POOL

Even if you are fortunate enough to live near the ocean or bay, there are many times when it's too cold or windy or brackish for comfortable swimming. And for many homes farther away from the coast, the convenience of a nice warm pool of one's own can be very compelling. While it's not quite the same as the ocean, it does bring to your doorstep a shimmering turquoise patch of water, which is refreshing and beautiful in and of itself. The options for pools are almost endless these

days, from the lavish infinity-edge pools and those with waterfalls and graduated edges, to smaller lap pools and plunge pools. And a hot tub or a whirlpool is always a welcome amenity for cooler nights, tired muscles, or romantic escapes.

CANVAS AWNING

Canvas awnings marching neatly across a facade and shading windows from the sun have long been a presence in many seaside communities. They offer a pleasing uniformity to a home; a softer form of architectural detail to plain-Jane exteriors; and the charm of a bygone era when people relied more on simple methods like shade to keep their homes cool. Larger awnings can also be employed to shade a porch or a terrace, with the flexibility of being retractable off-season or when not needed. Handsome as well as useful, awnings are deserving of a comeback.

WIDOW'S WALK

Ship captains' homes and those of other well-to-do seaport folks were often crowned by a widow's walk, a balustraded platform or lookout where the wife of a ship captain was said to pace as she watched and waited for her husband to return from sea (sometimes to no avail, hence the name). Widow's walks add great architectural character to a home, and nowadays are prized as an aerie from which to enjoy picturesque ocean or sunset vistas.

WEATHER VANE

Want to know which way the wind blows? Weather vanes have been an integral element in seaside communities for centuries, helping sailors gauge wind direction before heading out to sea. They also evolved into a highly valued form of folk art, so that weather-vane ornaments now are just as likely to be displayed inside as on top of the roof. In whimsical shapes such as sailboats and fish, they fulfill both aesthetic and practical purposes for homes by the water.

BEAD-BOARD PANELING

Once used in humble farmhouses as well as seaside cottages, bead board (also known as tongue-and-groove or wainscoting) is lately popular for the crisp white character it bestows on walls, providing more warmth and texture than plain Sheetrock. While bead board is particularly favored for kitchens and baths, it brings cottage charm to bedrooms, dining rooms, porch ceilings—almost any room of the home. Board-and-batten paneling is another, less ubiquitous, way to add architectural detail to a room.

accessories
SEASHELLS

These are the natural collections that we amass almost instinctively on walks along the shore. Souvenirs of many a vacation, talismans that the sea lets us borrow and carry home, shells have a natural beauty few purchased mementos can equal. They may be as common as a clamshell or as treasured as a conch or a whelk; gathered nearby or from far-flung destinations. Sand dollars, sea urchins, and starfish are prized specimens, too, and coral has become particularly fashionable. Living coral should never be removed from the ocean, however, and it is endangered, so buyer beware.

Shells can be gathered in a bowl or a tray, lined up on a mantel or a windowsill, or scattered across a table. Large shells and coral become an attractive display tucked into bookshelves or arrayed in a glass-fronted cupboard. Shadow boxes and display cases, whether antique or new, offer another interesting way to show off beachcombing finds.

Shells can be employed in a wide variety of subtle ways throughout a home: Tuck small votive candles into clamshells; use large scallop shells as dishes or saltcellars. Small shells with holes (available from craft stores) can be sewn to the edge of a curtain or the hem of a tablecloth. Strings of shells can become a beaded curtain. With glue gun in hand, you can easily affix shells to napkin rings, pushpins for a bulletin board, or hooks for a shower curtain; or decorate the frame of a mirror or a picture. A large shell makes a fine doorstop or bookend. The possibilities are numerous, and crafting with shells is always a good diversion for a rainy day at the beach.

SEA GLASS

The frosty translucence and luminous hues of sea glass make it a treasured

collectible, displayed inside a clear glass jar, nestled in a bowl, or even layered in a soap dish. Sea glass is becoming more rare, however, for a good reason: As people litter less, it washes up less frequently on shore. True sea glass is formed by glass bottles or items that have been hydrated and tumbled by the sea over the course of several years. Water leaches the lime and soda out of the glass, crystallizing the surface. Green, clear, and amber are the most common colors; gray, purple, and red are the rarest (red sea glass is supposedly found only once in every five thousand pieces). Sea glass can also be produced artificially in a rock tumbler or an acid bath, and can be purchased in bulk for crafts or display, but it won't have quite the same smoothness and crystal-etched surface.

SAILBOAT MODELS

There are few items that instantly say "beach" better than sailboat models. They might be pond yachts, miniature boats designed to be sailed with the wind like a sailboat; sailboat models made by boatbuilders or from kits; or half-block models, half-relief hull models carved by boat makers as part of the design process, and usually mounted on wood plaques. Even inexpensive wood toy sailboats add an unmistakably nautical flavor to any home. Try propping one up in a window or on a chest, or hang a series of half-block models on the wall to suggest a suitably maritime heritage.

SAILBOAT PHOTOGRAPHS

Gorgeous black-and-white photo-graphs of boats in full sail by such masters of the art as Beken of Cowes, and Morris and Stanley Rosenfeld (whose collection now belongs to the Mystic Seaport Museum), as well as many contemporary photographers, are compelling even to nonsailors. A framed set of prints, or if you have deep enough pockets, originals, bring hand-some beauty to a beach house, even if they are becoming something of a cliché. (Serious collectors should be sure to purchase only original vintage prints, not reprints from old negatives.) Those looking for something less expected might consider framing sailboat plans, illustrations of nautical knots, or vintage vacation brochures from seaside resorts.

SIGNAL FLAGS

These graphic elements up the seaworthy quotient of a home, whether

hung on a flagpole, in a banner across a porch, or framed on a wall. Swallowtail pennants and small triangular burgees are used as identifying flags for private boats and yacht clubs. Signal flags are an international code of forty flags—alphabetical and numerical—each of which has a distinct meaning. They can be hung singly, as a distress call, or in combination, for more elaborate messages. On special occasions, when vessels "dress ship," the international code flags are hung from bow to stern. The bright, primary-colored graphics of signal flags have made them popular imagery for everything from cocktail napkins and coffee mugs to needlepoint belts and throw pillows.

TROPHY FISH

A large stuffed marlin or sailfish on the wall may or may not be a genuine representation of your fishing prowess, but in an almost kitschy way, it is a vivid trophy of the sea. You can sometimes find fish at flea markets and garage sales, or if you are an authentic fisherman, have one of your own impressive catches stuffed and mounted. A fun tongue-in-cheek take on the trophy fish can be found painted in vibrant colors.

HURRICANE LANTERNS

Hurricane lanterns and oil lamps offer the romance of candlelight with shelter from the breeze. The flickering glow of candlelight creates the most appealing and intimate ambience for outdoor dining and summer evenings. Glass hurricanes and lanterns serve as clear sheaths to shelter large candles and refract the light. Oil lamps can be easily refilled and offer an adjustable flame. Tiki torches—small oil lanterns on stakes—can be placed around the perimeter of a patio or a lawn for a festive atmosphere. Use citronella oil in lanterns to help keep mosquitoes at bay.

NAUTICAL CHARTS AND COASTAL MAPS

Nautical charts and maps, particularly of the area where you live, make graphic, intriguing, and even useful art in a coastal home. You can find old maps on eBay or through antiques dealers, or new ones from boating stores and many online merchants. Framed on the wall, découpaged onto a tabletop or a tray, or perhaps used as wallpaper in a bath, they offer endless opportunity for geographical browsing.

PAINTINGS OF THE SEA

Maritime art and ship paintings have existed for centuries, often as documentation of particular ships, which were painted for the ship's captains, officers, or owners. There are many dealers and collectors of serious maritime art, but there's also beauty and pleasure to be found in flea-market paintings or contemporary artwork of sailboats, the ocean, and other shoreline settings. You will often find dealers of such art in beach towns (where their prices may reflect the tourist trade), but given that the sea is such a captivating subject, chances are you won't have to look far to find a painting that strikes your fancy.

MOSQUITO NETTING

With echoes of *Out of Africa* and tropical islands, white mosquito netting canopies have a gauzy, ethereal romance, but in some settings also serve the practical purpose of keeping out bugs. Mosquito netting is inexpensive

and easy to hang (most canopies are sewn onto a ring that can be hung from an eye hook in the ceiling), and it transforms a room instantly with soft femininity. You could also try hanging one above a daybed or even around a baby's crib.

PEG RACK

A peg rack is not unique to beach houses, of course, but it's what's hung on the pegs that creates a distinctly beachy vibe and easy, grab-and-go storage. Straw hats, beach bags, pareos, bathing suits, colorful beach towels, and baseball caps can all be there for the taking as you head out the door. Offer guests a little extra storage in a bedroom with a peg rack, try one in a bath, or use one to display a collection.

TELESCOPE AND BINOCULARS

These are not just props for decorating—every beach house worth its salt should have binoculars handy for viewing boats, birds,

and dolphins (or just trying to find family or friends on the beach), and perhaps a telescope for studying the stars. Vintage binoculars can make an aesthetic statement (and often still work), but have a pair of compact up-to-date ones on hand carry with you on outings.

AMERICAN FLAG

What would a beach house be without an American flag flying in the breeze? In addition to honoring our country, it's an instant indicator of which way the wind is blowing, and how strongly. Of course, you may choose to fly other flags as well, such as ones from a home country, yacht club, or college. But it's the stars and stripes that define the nautical palette, and our heritage.

MY FAVORITE BEACH-HOUSE SOURCES

Domestic Bliss
166 West Main Street
Mesa, AZ 85201
(480) 733-0552
www.domesticblissdesign.com

On the Veranda
4748 East Indian School Road
Phoenix, AZ 85018
(602) 955-8690
www.ontheveranda.net

Sage Antiques
335 West McDowell Road
Phoenix, AZ 85003
(602) 258-3033

CALIFORNIA

5 Seas
224 Marine Avenue
Balboa Island, CA 92662
(949) 673-1955
www.thefiveseas.com

Annie Magnolia
424 3rd Street
Eureka, CA 95501
(707) 268-1146

Anthropologie
1402 North Third Street Promenade
Santa Monica, CA 90401
(310) 393-4763
www.anthropologie.com

Antique Stove Heaven
5414 Western Avenue
Los Angeles, CA 90062
(323) 298-5581
www.antiquestoveheaven.com

Antonio's Bella Casa
322 North Newport Boulevard
Newport Beach, CA 92663
(949) 631-3416

Aris
1155 North Coast Highway
Laguna Beach, CA 92651
(949) 497-8300
www.arisonthecoast.com

Barclay Butera Furnishings & Interiors
169 North LaBrea Avenue
Los Angeles, CA 90036
(323) 634-0200

1745 Westcliff Drive
Newport Beach, CA 92660
(949) 650-8570
www.barclaybutera.com

Bark, Bath & Beyond
1330 South Coast Highway
Laguna Beach, CA 92651
(949) 715-3647
www.barkbathandbeyond.com

Bountiful
1335 Abbot Kinney Boulevard
Venice, CA 90291
(310) 450-3620
www.bountifulhome.com

Camps and Cottages
24000 Robinson Canyon Road
Carmel, CA 93923
(931) 622-0198
www.camps-cottages.com

Canyon Creek Nursery
3527 Dry Creek Road
Oroville, CA 95965
(530) 533-2166
www.canyoncreeknursery.com

The Chantel and Vicki Shoppe
432 East 17th Street
Costa Mesa, CA 92627
(949) 646-7506
www.thechantelandvickishoppe.com

D. Kruse
3412 Via Lido
Newport Beach, CA 92663
(949) 673-1302
www.d-kruse.com

Debra Huse Gallery
229 Marine Avenue, Suite E
Balboa Island, CA 92662
(949) 723-6171
www.debrahuse.com

Digging Dog Nursery
31101 Middle Ridge Road
Albion, CA 95410
(707) 937-1130
www.diggingdog.com

Flats Napa Valley
1154 Main Street
Saint Helena, CA 94574
(707) 967-0480
www.flatsnapavalley.com

Forget-Me-Nots
Sixth and Mission
P.O. Box 7318
Carmel, CA 93921
(831) 624-9080

Gatehouse
270 East 17th Street
Costa Mesa, CA 92627
(949) 515-2335
gatehouseinc@sbcglobal.net

Indigo Seas
123 North Robertson Boulevard
Los Angeles, CA 90048
(310) 550-8758

Island Home
313 Marine Avenue
Balboa Island, CA 92662
(949) 673-1133

Juxtaposition Home
7976 Pacific Coast Highway
Newport Coast, CA 92657
(949) 715-1181

Lala
1145 South Coast Highway
Laguna Beach, CA 92651
(949) 464-9220
www.kerrycassill.com

Les Interieurs
1701 Westcliff Drive
Newport Beach, CA 92660
(949) 650-7603
lesinterieurs@sbcglobal.net

Let's Go Shopping
114 Agate
Balboa Island, CA 92662
(949) 723-1169

Mélange
1235 North Coast Highway
Laguna Beach, CA 92651
(949) 497-4915

Michael Zschoche Gallery
209 Marine Avenue
Newport Beach, CA 92662
(949) 673-4255
www.mzgallery.net

Nobili Antiques
318 Old Newport Boulevard
Newport Beach, CA 92663
(949) 642-8402
nobili@earthlink.net

The Old Barn, Inc., Antiques Mall
31792 Camino Capistrano
San Juan Capistrano, CA 92675
(949) 493-9144

Olde Good Things
1800 South Grand Avenue
Los Angeles, CA 90015
(213) 746-8600
www.oldegoodthings.com

On Consignment
1190 Glenneyre
Laguna Beach, CA 92651
(949) 497-3700
treasures@onconsignment.org

Paula
139 West First Street, Suite B
Tustin, CA 92780
(877) 503-1856
www.shoppaula.com

Peter Blake Gallery
326 North Coast Highway
Laguna Beach, CA 92651
(949) 376-9994
www.peterblakegallery.com

PJ's Surfrider
2122 West Oceanfront
Newport Beach, CA 92663
(949) 673-1389
patl@pjssurfrider.com

Rachel Ashwell Shabby Chic
1013 Montana Avenue
Santa Monica, CA 90403
(310) 394-1975
www.shabbychic.com

Shirley's Heart
325 Marine Avenue
Balboa Island, CA 92662
(949) 675-4278
www.shirleysheart.com

Sommerska
324 Marine Island
Balboa Island, CA 92662
(949) 673-5707

Sydney Michelle
307 Marine Avenue
Balboa Island, CA 92662
(949) 673-2150
www.sydneymichelle.com

Talya Fashion Art
1259 South Coast Highway
Laguna Beach, CA 92651
(949) 715-3254
www.shoptalya.com

Teddy Bears and Tea Cups
225 Marine Avenue
Balboa Island, CA 92662
(949) 673-7204
www.teddybearsandteacups.com

Trove
1233 North Coast Highway
Laguna Beach, CA 92651
(949) 376-4640
www.trovelaguna.com

CONNECTICUT

The Antique and Artisan Center
69 Jefferson Street
Stamford, CT 06902
(203) 327-6022
www.stamfordantiques.com

Dovecote
56 Post Road East
Westport, CT 06880
(203) 222-7500

The Drawing Room
5 Suburban Avenue
Cos Cob, CT 06807
(203) 661-3737
www.thedrawingroom.com

Hiden Galleries
481 Canal Street
Stamford, CT 06902
(203) 323-9090
www.hiden-galleries-antiques.com

Nest
16 Stonington Road
Mystic, CT 06355
(860) 536-5400

FLORIDA

Bésame Mucho
315 Petronia Street
Key West, FL 33040
(305) 294-1928
www.besamemucho.net

Blue
718 Caroline Street
Key West, FL 33040
(305) 292-6268

Fonville Press
147 La Garza Lane
Alys Beach, FL 32413
(850) 213-5906
read2live@fonvillepress.com

House Key
810 Duval Street
Key West, FL 33040
(305) 295-6244
www.housekeyonline.com

Island Antiques
536 Fleming Street
Key West, FL 33040
(305) 294-0029

Jennifer Garrigues, Inc.
308 Peruvian Avenue
Palm Beach, FL 33480
(561) 659-7085
www.jennifergarrigues.com

Kemble Interiors, Inc.
294 Hibiscus Avenue
Palm Beach, FL 33480
(561) 659-5556
www.kembleinteriors.com

Key West Island Books
513 Fleming Street
Key West, FL 33040
(305) 294-2904
kwbook@aol.com

Lone Ranger Antiques
321 Walnut Street
Hollywood Beach, FL 33019
(954) 925-8990
www.lonerangerantiques.com

Magnolia
303 South Magnolia Avenue
Tampa, FL 33606
(813) 254-3337
www.magnoliastyle.com

Modica Market
109 Seaside Central Square
Santa Rosa Beach, FL 32459
(850) 231-1214
www.modicamarket.com

Pizitz Home and Cottage
P.O. Box 4670
Seaside, FL 32459
(866) 795-5675
(850) 231-2240

Sam's Treasure Chest
518 Fleming Street
Key West, FL 33040
(305) 296-5907

Scoop Beach
Shore Club Hotel
1901 Collins Avenue
Miami Beach, FL 33139
(305) 532-5929
www.scoopnyc.com

Sundog Books
89 Central Square
P.O. Box 4692
Santa Rosa Beach, FL 32459
(850) 231-5481
www.sundogbooks.com

GEORGIA

A. Tyner Antiques
200 Bennett Street NW
Atlanta, GA 30309
(404) 367-4484
www.swedishantiques.biz

MAINE

The Marston House
101 Main Street at Middle Street
P.O. Box 517
Wiscasset, ME 04578
(207) 882-6010
www.marstonhouse.com

MASSACHUSETTS

Brimfield Antique and Flea Market
Show
Brimfield, MA 01010
(413) 245-0030
www.brimfield.com

G.K.S. Bush, Inc.
13 Old South Road
Nantucket, MA 02554
(508) 325-0300

Midnight Farm
18 Water-Cromwell Lane
Vineyard Haven, MA 02568
(508) 693-1997
www.midnightfarm.net

Nantucket Country
38 Centre Street
Nantucket, MA 02554
(888) 411-8868
www.nantucketcountryantiques.com

NEW JERSEY

Gelco Woodcraft
1121 State Highway 35N
Ocean, NJ 07712
(732) 531-3800
www.gelcowoodcraft.com

Point Pleasant Antique Emporium
Bay and Trenton Avenue
Point Pleasant Beach, NJ 08742
(800) 322-8002

NEW MEXICO

The Ann Lawrence Collection
805 Early Street, Suite D
Santa Fe, NM 87501
(505) 982-1755
www.annlawrencecollection.com

Block Mercantile
418 Montezuma Avenue
Santa Fe, NM 87501
(505) 982-7477

Nathalie Home
241 Delgado
Santa Fe, NM 87501
(505) 992-1440
www.nathaliesantafe.com

NEW YORK

ABC Carpet and Home
888 and 881 Broadway
New York, NY 10003
(212) 473-3000
www.abchome.com

Air and Speed Surfshop
795 Montauk Highway
P.O. Box 2333
Montauk, NY 11954
(631) 668-0356

The American Wing
2415 Montauk Highway
P.O. Box 1131
Bridgehampton, NY 11932
(631) 537-3319
www.theamericanwing.com

Bagley Home
34 Main Street
Sag Harbor, NY 11963
(631) 725-3553

Balasses House
208 Main Street
P.O. Box 711
Amagansett, NY 11930
(631) 267-3032
balasses@optonline.net

Barbara Trujillo Antiques
2466 Main Street
P.O. Box 866
Bridgehampton, NY 11932
(631) 537-3838

Beall and Bell
18 South Street
Greenport, NY 11944
(631) 477-8239

Bittersweet Interiors
2442 Main Street
P.O. Box 662
Bridgehampton, NY 11932
(631) 537-5400

Bloom
43 Madison Street
Sag Harbor, NY 11963
(631) 725-5940

Broome Lampshades
325 Broome Street
New York, NY 10002
(212) 431-9666
www.lampshadesny.com

C&W Mercantile
Main Street
P.O. Box 1275
Bridgehampton, NY 11932
(631) 537-7914

Calypso Christiane Celle
24 Jobs Lane
Southampton, NY 11968
(631) 283-4321

Calypso Home
17 Newton Lane
East Hampton, NY 11937
(631) 324-8146

199 Lafayette Street
New York, NY 10013
(212) 925-6200
www.calypso-celle.com

Cottage
536 Main Street
East Quogue, NY 11942
(631) 653-9588

Croft Antiques
11 South Main Street
Southampton, NY 11968
(631) 283-6445

Dig Gardens
479 Atlantic Avenue
Brooklyn, NY 11217
(718) 554-0207
www.gardendig.com

English Country Antiques
Snake Hollow Road
Bridgehampton, NY 11932
(631) 537-0606
www.ecantiques.com

Equilibrium Surf Shop
Amagansett Square Village
Amagansett, NY 11930
(631) 267-6289

Harry Zarin
314 Grand Street
New York, NY 10002
(212) 925-6112
www.zarinfabrics.com

Hyman Hendler and Sons
67 West 38th Street
New York, NY 10018
(212) 840-8393
www.hymanhendler.com

Jamali Garden Supplies
149 West 28th Street
New York, NY 10001
(212) 244-4373
www.jamaligarden.com

Jarlathdan
255 Main Street
Amagansett, NY 11930
(631) 267-6455
www.jarlathdan.com

John Derian Company, Inc.
6 East Second Street
New York, NY 10003
(212) 677-3917
www.johnderian.com

Kathryn Nadeau Custom Framing
34 South Etna Avenue
P.O. Box 962
Montauk, NY 11954
(631) 668-6383

Laurin Copen Antiques
1703 Montauk Highway
P.O. Box 34
Bridgehampton, NY 11932
(631) 537-2802
www.laurincopenantiques.com

Linda and Howard Stein
2400 Montauk Highway
P.O. Box 1276
Bridgehampton, NY 11932
(631) 537-8848
www.lindahowardstein.com

Liza Sherman
112 Hampton Street
Sag Harbor, NY 11963
(631) 725-1437

Marsia Holzer Studio
399 Washington Street
New York, NY 10013
(212) 431-9343
www.marsiaholzer.com
By appointment only

Martell's Stationery and Gifts
880 Main Street
Montauk, NY 11954
(631) 668-1248

Melet Mercantile
84 Wooster Street
New York, NY 10012
(212) 925-8353
By appointment only

Nellie's of Amagansett
230 Main Street
P.O. Box 2790
Amagansett, NY 11930
(631) 267-1000

Neo-Studio
25 Madison Street
Sag Harbor, NY 11963
(631) 725-6478
neo-studio@earthlink.net

Olde Good Things
124 West 24th Street
New York, NY 10011
(888) 551-7333
www.oldegoodthings.com

Paula Rubenstein
65 Prince Street
New York, NY 10012
(212) 966-8954

Polo Country Store
31-33 Main Street
East Hampton, NY 11937
(631) 324-1222
www.polo.com

R.E. Steele Antiques
74 Montauk Highway, Unit 11
East Hampton, NY 11937
(631) 324-7812

Ralph Lauren
41 Jobs Lane
Southampton, NY 11968
(631) 287-6953
www.polo.com

Ruby Beets
25 Washington Street
P.O. Box 1174
Sag Harbor, NY 11963
(631) 899-3275
www.rubybeets.com

Sage Street Antiques
Corner of Rte. 114 and Sage Street
Sag Harbor, NY 11963
(631) 725-4036
Weekends only

Scoop Beach
47 Newtown Lane
East Hampton, NY 11937
(631) 329-8080
www.scoopnyc.com

The Shop
504 East 74th Street
New York, NY 10021
(877) 466-7467
www.theshopnyny.com

Simon's Hardware and Bath
421 Third Avenue
New York, NY 10016
(212) 532-9220
www.simons-hardware.com

Sylvester and Co.
Main Street
P.O. Box 2069
Sag Harbor, NY 11963
(631) 725-5012
sylvesterco@verizon.net

Sylvester and Co. at Home
154 Main Street
P.O. Box 7090
Amagansett, NY 11930
(631) 267-9777
www.sylvesterathome.com

Sylvester and Co. Essentials
146 Main Street
P.O. Box 7090
Amagansett, NY 11930
(631) 267-7707
www.sylvesteressentials.com

Tauk
54 South Erie Avenue
P.O. Box 1677
Montauk, NY 11954
(631) 668-3686
tauk@earthlink.net

Treillage Ltd.
418 East 75th Street
New York, NY 10021
(212) 535-2288
www.treillageonline.com

Tutto Bene
2414 Main Street
P.O. Box 1156
Bridgehampton, NY 11932
(631) 537-3320

Zoom
10 Job's Lane
Southampton, NY 11968
(631) 283-9216

NORTH CAROLINA

Summerhouse
1722 Battleground Avenue
Greensboro, NC 27408
(336) 275-9655
www.summerhousestores.com

OREGON

Rejuvenation
1100 Southeast Grand Avenue
Portland, OR 97214
(888) 401-1900
www.rejuvenation.com

Sesame and Lilies
183 North Hemlock
Cannon Beach, OR 97110
(503) 436-2027

Highway 101 and Pacific Way
52 South Park Drive
Gearhart, OR 97138
(503) 738-7137
www.sesameandlilies.com

Starr Antique Mall
7027 Southeast Milwaukie Avenue
Portland, OR 97202
(503) 239-0346
www.starsantique.com

RHODE ISLAND

House
152 Mill Street
Newport, RI 02840
(401) 847-9879

TEXAS

Antique Warehouse
423 Rosenberg
Galveston, TX 77550
(409) 762-8620

Indulge
2903 Saint Street
Houston, TX 77027
(713) 888-0181

Leftovers Antique Destination
3900 Highway 290 West
Brenham, TX 77833
(979) 830-8496

The Original Round Top
Antiques Fair
P.O. Box 180
Smithville, TX 78957
(512) 237-4747
www.roundtopantiquesfair.com
Show in April and October in Round
Top, Texas

Room Service by Ann Fox
4354 Lovers Lane
Dallas, TX 75225
(214) 369-7666
www.roomservicehome.com

Shabby Slips
2304 Bissonett
Houston, TX 77005
(713) 630-0066
www.shabbyslipshouston.com

The Sitting Room
6213 Edloe
Houston, TX 77005
(713) 523-1925
www.thesittingroom.net

UTAH

Nature's Pressed, Inc.
P.O. Box 212
Orem, UT 84059
(800) 850-2499
www.naturespressed.com

VIRGINIA

Brent and Becky's Bulbs
7900 Daffodil Lane
Gloucester, VA 23061
(877) 661-2852
www.brentandbeckysbulbs.com

ACKNOWLEDGMENTS

For Reg and Cinco—my beach buddies.

And, always to Samantha Emmerling and Jonathan Emmerling, Terry Ellisor, and all my best friends in the Hamptons for thirty years of fabulous beach parties, especially the one where we almost lost Terry! And all our thanks to Juanita Jones, who always kept the beach houses going.

To the two most wonderful weddings on the beach—Samantha's wedding to Sam Henning at her father's Cape Cod house on the beach, and Jonathan's wedding to Betsey McCall in Key West, Florida, the most fun beach town in the USA.

Many thanks to Carter Berg for the fabulous photographs and all the fun and miles we put on the rental cars.

Thanks to designer Vanessa Holden; Aliza Fogelson, my editor at Clarkson Potter; and Jill Kirchner Simpson, who brought all my beach dreams to life in a beautifully designed and written book. And to Jane Treuhaft, Maggie Hinders, Sibylle Kazeroid, Joan Denman, and Lindsay Miller for your care in making sure every detail was right.

Much appreciation to Gayle Benderoff, for standing by me all these many years we have been doing books together. And to Carol Sama Sheehan,

Jen Kopf, Jane Perdue, and the whole staff at Country Home, who are always so supportive.

And, of course, my greatest thanks to the many home owners and friends who let us into their beautiful beach houses and generously shared with us their favorite stories, memories, and adventures at the beach (and for those that ended up on the cutting-room floor, I am truly sorry!). Also to the many kind and helpful people who gave us leads and introduced us to new friends: Lynn Sherman and Leonard Reiss; Shirley and Kirby Fortenberry; Liz and Michael Pierce; Rachel Ashwell; Barclay Butera; Ginger Barber; Suzy and Richard Grote; Bob, Pam, and Sunny Melet; Marsia and Leonard Holzer; Fiona Duff Kahn and Robert Kahn; Debbie and Rod Canada; Dee and Randy Kruse; Lenny and Bob Steinberg; Hanna Struever; DD Allen; Peter Blake; Ted and Jacqueline Miller; Jeffree Turney, aka the Long Ranger; Shannon Bowers; Pam Pierce; Jennifer and John Saucer; Cindy David; Carol Glasser; Patti Kenner; Lee Sable; Clarissa Block; David Simon of Blue in Fort Lauderdale; Joyce and Rod Wilson in Watercolor, Florida; Kim Chosen; Liz Garrett; Wendy Riva; Doug Bihlmaier; and Jill Goldman.

I couldn't have written this book without you! When you are all on a beach and there is a full moon, think of me.